Single Adoptive Parents: Our Stories

Single Adoptive Parents: Our Stories

By

Sherry Fine & Lee Varon

www.bookstandpublishing.com

Published by
Bookstand Publishing
Morgan Hill, CA 95037
3634_2

ISBN 978-1-61863-274-6

Printed in the United States of America

Disclaimer: All stories in this book are based on real people but
their names and identifying information have been changed to
protect privacy. Some of these stories are based on composite
characters.

CONTENTS

The following chapters are based on feedback obtained through our surveys and our clinical experience.

Friends, Family and Support Networks

Initial reactions and ongoing effects on relationships with friends and family. Also a look at developing a support network as a single adoptive parent. We look at various and creative coping mechanisms and identify some of the unique challenges posed for families created by single parent adoption.

Juggling Career and Parenting

Juggling the demands of working and parenting on the income of one person. We will look at coping mechanisms and identify some of the unanticipated costs that may arise.

Special Needs of Single Adoptive Families

This chapter highlights the Special Needs of Single Adoptive Families. In addition, it will offer suggestions for those in the midst of raising their children, as well as those contemplating single parent adoption.

Joys

This chapter looks at the many joys single adoptive parents have experienced and wanted to share.

Our Children Speak Out

This chapter is a collection of unedited commentaries by (now) adult adoptees of single parents.

PREFACE

Most of us are well aware of the hardships, struggles, joys, and celebrations that parenting brings. Having a child, either through birth or through adoption, is a risk. Single parents and adoptive parents will have different and often additional needs as compared to a two-parent family with birth children. If you are in the decision making stage we hope this book will help you decide whether adopting as a single parent is right for you. If you have already adopted and are in the process of raising your child(ren), we hope this book will provide support and guidance for your family.

We do not wish to encourage nor discourage individuals to become single adoptive parents. However, what we do hope to convey is an honest account of the experience of being a single adoptive parent. Our material is based on responses to our questionnaire and interviews with single adoptive parents. They offer words of advice to prospective single adoptive parents who are contemplating this life changing decision. We will share the experiences of a group of adult adoptees, all of whom were adopted as young children by single parents, and all willing to share bits of their life stories. These are individual and unique stories and reflect only their personal experiences.

viii

CHAPTER ONE

Vignettes

The Decision

In 1984, we, Sherry and Lee, were both single adoptive parents. Sherry had adopted seven year old Jackie from Colombia and two year old Alfonso from El Salvador. Lee had just arrived home from El Salvador with her eight month old son, Jose. Both social workers, we had met during the course of adopting our children and became friends. Although we were both overjoyed with our newly formed families, we soon came to realize that there were many challenges that lay ahead. We understood how important support would be while raising our children. Although we were fortunate to have one another and the support of a larger circle of single adoptive parents, we realized that not everyone had access to this kind of network and so we created a counseling and consulting agency, "The Adoption Network," and developed an eight-week workshop focusing on decision-making for single people exploring adoption. In this workshop, we covered issues including how adoption impacts relationships, as well as issues of employment, finances, support networks, adoption vs. biological parenting, and fertility. We also addressed the logistics of the adoption home study and agencies. The following vignettes are based on people who responded

1

to our survey for single adoptive parents and participants in our workshops.

Sarah – 1981 (Adopted when she was 40)

My biological clock was ticking…

"I couldn't believe it! Forty years old, unmarried and without a child!"

Sarah had always imagined that one day she would marry and have children. A teacher for twenty years, she was well-loved by students and parents alike, and well-respected by her colleagues. She had had several relationships and twice had hopes that these would lead to marriage.

"My last relationship ended just before my fortieth birthday. Brad and I dated on and off for three years. He knew how much I wanted a family, and I was becoming increasingly frustrated with his unwillingness to commit. As my frustration grew, he became more distant. One day it dawned on me that I was wasting my time. We had done some great traveling together and we both loved to ski and scuba dive. He was six years younger than me and I realized he wanted to continue this lifestyle, but I was ready for a change. He really didn't want to be tied down with kids. For years I had hung on hoping things would change. I knew it was time to move on but where was I going?"

Sarah, like so many single women we have worked with, had come to a point in her life where her focus had shifted. She was looking for someone who was ready to settle down and start a family.

"After ending the relationship with Brad, I dated a few men but each one I went out with I saw only as a potential candidate for fatherhood. Was he good with kids? Did he have a stable job? Looking back, I don't blame these guys for running in the other direction. I just wanted to skip the courtship and start looking for cribs and car seats. My biological clock was ticking and that's the only sound I could hear."

Sarah had a large extended family and looked forward to spending holidays with them. Her younger sister was married and recently had a child. Although Sarah was happy for her sister, the birth of her niece served to intensify her own sense of loss. Family gatherings had become increasingly stressful, especially when relatives pressed her with questions about her social life.

"Forty was a turning point in my life. In retrospect, the year after I turned forty was probably the most difficult one I can remember. I gained a lot of weight and withdrew from some of my closest friends. I now know I was depressed and felt that marriage and family – that great American dream I had grown up believing – was not going to happen for me."

Sarah went through a process of grieving. She struggled with the reality of being a single woman who wanted to be married with children, yet she found herself facing the future alone.

"I decided to see a counselor who helped me to sort out my feelings. I realized that although I wanted to be both married and a mother, of the two, motherhood was far more important. I just couldn't see my life without a child. Once I realized this, the search for a partner went flying out the window and I began to explore my options."

Sarah had heard about women who had made the decision to parent on their own and found various ways to conceive. She considered this option but did not want to go through a pregnancy alone.

"In the past I had thought about having a child with a partner by my side. Once I started thinking about parenting on my own, I felt being pregnant without a partner would only intensify my feelings of loneliness."

In the absence of a loving relationship, the need to have a biological child was clearly not as compelling. Through all of her years of teaching, Sarah had loved and nurtured her students. She knew there were thousands of children waiting to be adopted and she felt capable of loving one of them.

"Suddenly, I was obsessed with learning more about adoption. I went to my local library and found a large notebook that had pictures and biographies of children waiting to be adopted. I fell in love with a three year old biracial girl, Denise. Her social worker's number was listed right under her picture. I rushed right home and called. The information I received that afternoon would dash my hopes of becoming Denise's mother and begin the roller coaster ride that would eventually lead me to bring home my daughter."

Sarah learned that most social workers were looking for two-parent homes. In the early '80s the hierarchy of adoptive parent applicants placed singles on the bottom rung. At that time, transracial adoptions were controversial for Caucasians like Sarah seeking to adopt African American and biracial children. Domestic adoption options for would-be single parents were generally limited to older children or those with special needs. Nevertheless, Sarah decided to make an appointment with the state social service agency. What she heard next would change her course.

"The social worker explained that it was rare for healthy children below the age of five to be placed with single people through the state social service agency. My heart was really set on a younger child, but I wanted to be flexible. Although I was ready and anxious to be a mom, I felt an older child with a difficult history would be a challenge even for a stable two- parent family. The social worker encouraged me to look into private agencies, as there would be a wider network of resources available."

Sarah called a number of private agencies. The first one she called was cordial but they openly admitted they had never placed a child with a single person before. However, as she continued her search, she found an agency that was welcoming and supportive. The options were few, however they included younger minority children from Texas as well as international programs in India and El Salvador.

Sarah considered an African American child from Texas. However, her close African American friend dissuaded her since she felt that children should be placed with a family of the same race. Sarah considered her friend's advice and decided that it might be difficult for an African American child to be raised by a single white woman in the United States. Sarah had traveled extensively throughout South America, spoke Spanish and felt comfortable with the Latino culture. She learned that the program in El Salvador was moving smoothly and rapidly and was accepting single applicants. Her decision was made. Three weeks later she received a picture of her eight month old daughter, Graciela.

In our years running groups for single people interested in adoption we have come across many stories like Sarah's. Such themes as turning forty or an approaching birthday that draws attention to one's ticking biological clock, hearing about a friend or family member becoming pregnant, the end of a relationship or the realization that they may not find a partner with whom to parent, were common triggers which led people to our groups.

Linda – 1975 (Adopted when she was 32)

I just wanted to make a difference…

Linda, 32, began thinking about adoption in her teens. "I remember reading an article in the *Tribune* about a single woman adopting a child on her own. The

6

article grabbed my attention and I just knew one day I would do the same."

After graduating from college, Linda took a job as a social worker in a state social service agency. She loved her work and assisted with the adoption of many children. Linda attended church regularly, and did a lot of outreach work with children in the community.

"I started a Big Brothers Big Sisters Program at my church and became a Big Sister to a little girl named Alice. Alice was living with her grandmother since her mom had been incarcerated on drug-related charges. I remember the joy I felt taking her home on Christmas Eve to meet my family. I come from a large extended family with lots of nieces and nephews. Alice was thrilled with all the attention and presents she received that night. We saw each other weekly and on occasion she slept over at my house. We saw a lot of movies and ate a lot of ice cream."

"It hit me real hard when Alice's mom was released from prison and they moved out of state. I was startled by the emotional impact of her move and realized how attached I was to this little girl. Although we stayed in touch with letters and phone calls, it just wasn't the same. I began to realize how important it was for me to have an ongoing relationship with a child."

While many of her friends were getting married and beginning families, Linda had little interest in dating.

"I had a few blind dates but they never seemed to go anywhere. I was a child of the sixties. In my early twenties, I just wanted to make a difference in the world. In my early thirties, I was considering joining the Peace Corps when my life suddenly took a different direction."

The agency Linda worked for was having difficulty finding a placement for two Caucasian brothers, Richie, five and Jessie, three. Both boys had experienced the loss of their young mother and they had been diagnosed with ADHD. They had already been in three foster homes and the agency was having difficulty finding an adoptive home where they could be placed together. Despite the loss of their mother, the boys were resilient and shared a strong sibling bond.

"I couldn't bear to see them separated," Linda said. "I realized that I was becoming very invested in seeing what happened to these boys and even began to fantasize about adopting them."

Linda's agency had begun to place children with single parents although it was still a rare occurrence. Linda knew the boys' social worker and approached her after her weekly staff meeting. It was clear, that despite their difficult history, the social worker felt the boys had a lot of potential but desperately needed a consistent, structured and loving home. Their mother had raised the boys as a single parent and had been devoted to them until her untimely death from complications of diabetes. The father, who had left after Jessie was born, had terminated all parental rights. The social worker felt that a single female would be a good placement for the boys and above all, she did not want to see them separated.

"After my conversation with the social worker," said Linda, "I couldn't get the boys out of my mind."

Finances are often a major stumbling block for single people considering adoption. Linda's salary as a social worker covered her expenses and a few luxuries, like travel. However she was still paying off student loans and living in a studio apartment. She realized her life would undergo many changes if she were going to become a family of three. Because of the boys' status as "waiting children" they would both be receiving financial subsidies and medical coverage. Despite this, Linda felt the financial commitment would be overwhelming.

"I decided not to pursue the adoption but was left with an empty place in my heart."

Paula was a good friend of Linda's. She and her husband had children both by birth and adoption. Linda confided in Paula about her sadness at feeling unable to adopt Jessie and Richie. Paula encouraged her not to give up and together they discussed the steps she would need to take before going forward with the adoption. The first thing Linda did was to approach her parents.

"I knew they had put aside some money for wedding expenses for me and my two sisters. I told them how much I wanted to adopt and asked them if they would be willing to give me the money in advance. I told them that I didn't know if I would ever marry but I did know that I wanted to adopt some day. I didn't tell them I was interested in a sibling pair. I thought they would flip out."

To her amazement, Linda's parents were more receptive than she expected. They were willing to give her what they had set aside for her although they still hoped she would find a husband.

The next step that Linda took was to approach her supervisor for a raise. She had been in the same position for three years with an excellent record and felt she had earned a promotion.

"Although I had been timid in the past, the hope of adopting the boys gave me the courage to ask my boss for a raise. My legs were trembling as I had never asserted myself in this way before."

Linda's boss was supportive but unable to promote her to the supervisory position she had hoped for. He did, however, offer her a small increase. With his support, the support of her parents and her friend Paula, Linda decided she was able to move forward.

Her last hurdle was her living situation. She couldn't accommodate the boys in her small studio.

"If I were to adopt the boys I would need a larger apartment in a community with a better school system."

The boys' social worker was willing to complete Linda's home study since she knew Linda was looking for a larger place. Fortunately, once she shared her housing dilemma with others, a friend from church told her about a two-bedroom apartment in a two-family home in exactly the area she wanted to move to. "That very day I went over to look at the apartment and it was perfect. It had a large porch and a small backyard and was just three blocks from the school I hoped the boys could attend! The elderly landlord was pleased to hear I loved to garden. She was willing to reduce the already reasonable rent even further in exchange for upkeep of the yard. I was thrilled! I felt this was meant to be - all signs pointed to my becoming the mother of Jessie and Richie!"

Although finances can be a major concern, creative solutions can often be found for those who are strongly motivated to parent. In our groups for single people who are considering adoption, we have heard a wide array of solutions for those for whom finances are an issue. Among these solutions are: taking out a loan, throwing a pre-adoption party, having a roommate or moving closer to family. While the cost of adoption can be considerable, there are options such as the foster-adopt program where expenses are minimal or non-existent. Foster-adopt programs are domestic adoption programs where a child is placed in a home as a foster child with the hope and expectation that the child will become legally available for adoption.

At the point of considering adoption, individuals will often express the sentiment that they have fulfilled many of their dreams including academic pursuits and travel, and are now ready to settle down to create a home with a child.

Jill – 1995 (Adopted when she was 46)

My life was my work…

Jill, a 46 year old Director of Marketing for a large firm, had focused on her demanding career throughout her adult life.

"I think my father's early death when I was seven years old, and the change in our financial standing, drove me to later achieve financial independence. My mom, a secretary, was left destitute after my dad suddenly died of a heart attack at the age of 47. We had to rely on my aunt and uncle to pull us through."

"In the '70s more opportunities were opening up for women in the business world. I became a poster child for women executives and even had my name in *Cosmopolitan* as a woman who had made over $100,000."

Although Jill dated sporadically and thought one day she would like to have children, she hadn't met anyone she wanted to marry. When Jill was 45, her mother suffered a stroke and Jill had to come to terms with the knowledge that her mother wouldn't be around forever. An only child, Jill came from a very small family. Along with her mother, her aunt and uncle were her only immediate relatives.

"After my Mom's stroke, the importance of family took on new meaning. Everyone in my immediate family was in their 80s and I was struck by the realization that if I didn't have children, my family would end with me, and no one would inherit the memories and traditions of our family."

By her mid-forties, Jill still had not met a man she wanted to marry. She realized that if she was to become a mother, she would be doing it solo. Her religious beliefs precluded her from considering becoming pregnant as a single person, so adoption seemed to be the path to motherhood.

"Suddenly, the goal of becoming the first female VP of my company took a backseat to my desire to parent. Once I began exploring adoption there was no turning back. My organizational skills that served me so well in my career were focused on my search for a child. Given my age, I was concerned that I might be too old to adopt a younger child. I was ecstatic when I learned that my age would not be a barrier in China.[1] The home study was going well and after three sessions with my adoption social worker, I was given a picture of seven month old Kim."

For many single people career can become an all-consuming part of their lives. When considering adoption as a single parent, priorities need to be readjusted. At times, demanding schedules need to be reassessed given the needs of a child.

---

[1] As of this writing, China is no longer accepting single applicants. Since 1983, we have continued to witness countries and specific programs both open and close their doors to singles.

We have worked with prospective adoptive parents ranging in age from their twenties to their fifties, but the majority has been in their thirties and forties. Although an older parent may bring the assets of wisdom, maturity and financial stability, there can be challenges as well. The everyday physical demands of a young child can be difficult when dealing with a diminishing level of energy as one ages. An older parent adopting a younger child must additionally consider that the child's peers will likely have much younger parents. Jill had considered these issues.

"At 46, I felt I had enough energy to raise a child. Luckily I had financial resources and planned to hire some help. I decided to take early retirement and build my own consulting practice. In this way I would have the flexibility to spend time with my daughter."

The agency Jill was working with, had introduced her to many families who had adopted from China. She found a wealth of information and support among this network of people.

While Jill felt comfortable with her decision to adopt, she still hadn't broken the news to her family. She realized she was worried about their reaction. Ever since her father's death, her mother, aunt and uncle had been very protective of her, and she felt they might not understand why a single woman would want to raise a child, particularly a child of a different ethnicity. Their parochial views bothered her, but she believed they had her best interests at heart.

Jill's concerns were confirmed when she finally announced to her family her plans to adopt. They were upset about Jill raising a child of another race. In addition, they worried because they didn't think she could manage on her own, especially if they weren't around to help.

"My uncle was more negative than my mom and my aunt. He actually told me that adopting would ruin my life and that someday my child would end up hating me. I felt defeated after my uncle's tirade. My mom just gave me the silent treatment. I was on my own. Kim was beautiful. I was overjoyed and shared her picture with everyone I knew, even the mailman! But I felt I couldn't share it with my own family and that was a huge disappointment."

Jill felt her aunt would be more receptive than either her mother or her uncle. She decided to take her aunt out to lunch with Kim's picture in hand.

"I told my aunt how much this meant to me, that it wasn't a frivolous decision, but one I had contemplated for a long time. I also assured her that I was developing a support network and would hire someone to help me with my child. She smiled when she saw Kim's picture. Although I knew she had reservations she was willing to support me all the way, as she had always done in the past. She promised me she would speak to my mom and uncle and would do her best to soften their attitudes."

Many singles considering adoption are faced with skepticism and/or criticism from friends and family, although most negative feelings lessen with time. Jill avoided talking about the adoption with her mother and uncle whom she believed would be negative about her decision. Dealing with others, particularly those who are critical, during this emotionally taxing period, adds additional stressors to the process. It may be helpful to begin discussing plans to adopt with those who you feel may be more open or at least neutral about your desire to adopt.

Grace – 1985 (Adopted when she was 36)
Could I love an adopted child?

"I always knew I would be a mom but I had never considered adoption." Grace, 36, said: "My mom raised me and my two sisters as a single parent and I never doubted for a minute that I was capable of doing the same."

A primary care doctor by profession, Grace always planned to conceive a child in her thirties whether or not she was in a relationship. She had a good friend who was raising a child on her own, and introduced Grace to the local chapter of *Single*

Mothersby Choice[2]. After attending one of their meetings, she was encouraged by the group and motivated to begin the process.

She had it all planned out. She would conceive with an anonymous donor and hopefully be pregnant during the spring and deliver by late fall or early winter. After several months of unsuccessful insemination attempts, Grace decided to make an appointment with a fertility specialist. She found out that her fallopian tubes were damaged and surgery was recommended. The surgery went smoothly but it took several months to recover. Eventually, Grace became pregnant but had an ectopic pregnancy, and nearly hemorrhaged to death.

"I was devastated but determined. IVF (in vitro fertilization) was a new technology but it was my only hope. Despite the fact that insurance would not cover the treatment, I forged ahead. The red hair that had been in my family for generations and the keen intellect were traits that I hoped to pass on to my child. In fact, the donors I had chosen were successful and well-educated. To be honest, I was unwilling to give up the image of my ideal child."

After three unsuccessful IVF cycles, Grace had nearly exhausted her savings and felt demoralized as

---

[2] *Single Mothers by Choice* is an organization that was founded in 1981 by Jane Mattes, C.S.W., a psychotherapist and single mother by choice. Their mission is to provide support and information to single women who are considering, or who have chosen, single motherhood.

though her body had been ravaged. It was her mother that suggested Grace look into adoption. "'Never!' was my first thought."

During the following year, Grace came to terms with the reality that she would never be able to conceive a child. The IVF process was financially, physically and emotionally exhausting. "For a while I decided I would forego the possibility of parenting. This thought left me feeling empty, but I just didn't know if I could be a good parent to an adopted child."

"Two years passed. I worked. I traveled. I went out with friends. I tried to go on with my life, but I always felt something was missing. One day a new patient, a woman in her forties, mentioned that she was going to Ukraine to adopt a child. She seemed overjoyed and took out a picture of an adorable Ukrainian toddler. I was surprised at the rush of feeling that overcame me!"

"The image of that little girl stayed with me and two weeks later I decided to join a group of prospective single adoptive parents run by *The Adoption Network*[3]. It was led by two social workers, both single adoptive parents. I finally found a place to be open and share my story. I was amazed at how strong my emotions were. All the pent up anger, sadness and longing suddenly overcame me and uncharacteristically, I began to cry.

---

[3] *The Adoption Network* was founded in 1984 by Sherry Fine LCSW, and Lee Varon, LICSW, psychotherapists and single adoptive parents.

The group was incredibly supportive and over the next few weeks proved a safe haven to work through my feelings. I had the information I needed and was ready to move forward. Once I worked through my initial discomfort, I began to tell everyone I knew that I was interested in adoption. I was still however feeling the need to adopt a child as young as possible. I was even hoping to breastfeed, as crazy as that seemed to most people. Because I knew I wanted an infant, I approached an agency that worked with birthmothers. My social worker was candid and told me that few Caucasian babies were available for adoption, especially for single people. She informed me, that on occasion, those children who were harder to place because of their race or special needs might be available to singles."

Grace continued to explore her options and told everyone she knew that she was interested in adopting an infant. One day, another doctor and colleague called Grace with the news of a young pregnant woman who was raised by a single mom. She was open to placing her child in a single parent home, however her main criteria was finding someone who would accept an open adoption so that she could have ongoing contact with her child. The young woman was Caucasian and her boyfriend was African American. Grace's colleague set up a meeting between her and the young woman.

"I was so nervous I could hardly wait," said Grace. "When the day came, I drove to meet Tammy. She was a sweet young girl who had just turned seventeen and wanted to complete her high school education and go on to college. Although we were both anxious, I was impressed with her maturity. She was in counseling and had reached the point where she felt adoption was the best decision for her and her child. Her boyfriend agreed with her decision."

When Grace met Tammy she felt an instant rapport although she had many questions about open adoption. After talking to her agency's social worker, Grace called Tammy and asked if she would like to meet with herself and the social worker. Tammy agreed to the meeting and added that she would be bringing her mother. Open adoption was appealing to Tammy's mother. She would not lose touch with her grandchild. Furthermore, she was relieved knowing her grandchild would be well cared for. In addition, the father of Tammy's baby was not ready to be a parent but cared for Tammy and wanted to make sure their child was raised in a good home. He too was open to having contact with the child at some point in the future.

Although initially Grace had a strong desire to give birth and raise a child that reflected her genetic traits, after arduous fertility treatments, she realized this would not be possible. She was able to work these issues through and moved on to adoption. She had always dreamed of holding her child immediately after birth. In addition, she felt reassured being able to know the birthparents and why they chose adoption for their child. She felt she had better access to her child's medical background by having an ongoing relationship with her child's birthmother.

Tammy gave birth to a seven-pound baby boy who Grace named Matthew. Tammy gave the child his middle name, Shawn. Grace and Tammy, along with the adoption social worker, agreed to bi-annual visits and ongoing check-ins.

While some fear the contact that comes with an open adoption, others like Grace prefer having contact with birthparents. A study in the 2003 *Child Welfare Gateway Bulletin* (published by the US Department of Health and Human Services) indicates that the fear that birthmothers will attempt to reclaim their children is largely a myth. Furthermore, most children in open adoptions are not confused about who their parents are, and they do understand the different roles of adoptive and birthparents. Questions such as, "Who am I?" and "Where did I come from?" are often easier for a child in an open adoption to answer. Open adoption often helps children integrate past and present and develop a more integrated sense of their identity.

For some, the desire for a biological child is strong. Like Grace, they may have a clear image of their child. While Grace was able to resolve the sense of loss associated with the inability to conceive and go on to successfully adopt a child, it is not possible for others. The importance of resolving the loss of having a biological child is important to address. Furthermore, most adoption agencies will recommend that a client has reached some closure regarding their desire to parent a child by birth before moving forward with an adoption.

Sandra – 1990 (Adopted when she was 42)

Cancer was the wake-up call…

Sandra, a 42 year old African American woman, had been married and divorced in her mid-twenties. An English professor at a well-respected university, she had been consumed by her career and devoted little time to her personal life. Following her divorce, she threw herself with even greater intensity into her work.

"I felt like my work was my only salvation," Sandra said. She received numerous awards and tenure at her university. She was being considered for the position of Dean of Students when she received the shock of her life - she was diagnosed with cancer. "I felt as though I was run over by a speeding train. For several months, all I could focus on was healing myself. This included chemotherapy and a complete hysterectomy. My family, my mom and my sister, lived on the opposite coast and I considered relocating to be near them. However, I really enjoyed my job and the people I worked with. Despite support from friends and family during my illness, I felt very lonely. My illness compelled me to re-evaluate my life. During my marriage, my husband and I had always planned on having children. When the marriage dissolved, I abandoned thoughts of a family. I had never thought much about having a family on my own, but suddenly, when the possibility of having one was taken away, I was surprised at the intensity of this loss."

The doctors told Sandra that if she could make it through the next five years, she would have a good chance of living a normal life, cancer-free. The next several years were spent on a rigorous regimen of diet, exercise and researching alternative therapies. She came out of that period with a sense of gratitude and a commitment to live life to its fullest.

Sandra did not want to abandon the hope of becoming a mother but as she celebrated her fifth year of living cancer-free, she realized both her age and her medical history precluded her from considering biological parenting. Increasingly, she felt a strong desire to parent a child and began to explore her options. As an African-American woman she believed she would have no difficulty adopting a young child. However, Sandra was more interested in adopting an older child. "At this point in my life," said Sandra, "I was accustomed to having a great deal of freedom and felt I would be a better parent to an older child."

Sandra was always interested in the newspaper column listing children waiting to be adopted and at times, had almost picked up the phone to find out more. She knew many adoption agencies were looking for African-American parents, especially for older children. However, she hesitated calling because of her medical history.

"I shared my desire to parent as well my anxiety with my oncologist. He said he would be willing to write a letter confirming my positive prognosis if needed. At the same time, my sister, who had been a foster parent for many years, sent me an article about a single woman who had been cancer-free for many years and had adopted a sibling group. It was clear that agencies were becoming more flexible, particularly in the placement of children waiting to be adopted."

Sandra realized that if she were to adopt a child, she would need to expand her support network. While she had many close friends, some of whom had children, she knew few adoptive families, and even fewer women who were parenting on their own. She called her sister who referred Sandra to her own social worker. That social worker connected Sandra to a local agency where she made an appointment and her first step toward adoption.

"I was nervous about meeting my social worker, but in fact she was a lovely elderly woman who put me at ease immediately and assured me that if I decided to adopt, there was a child for me. We went on to discuss my health issues, and although she assured me that adoption was possible, she said it was critical to address several issues. She pointed out that it would be important to check the provisions of my disability insurance and appoint a guardian. I left her office with the intent to update my will and a plan to broaden my support network. Over the next several weeks I made contact with a single adoptive parents' group and connected with the single parents' group at my church. Although most of the single parents were divorced, some had chosen to parent on their own. . They welcomed me into their midst and I began attending their weekly potluck dinners, and monthly outings. I felt I had found the support I needed to move forward."

Often, single people consider adopting an older child. Many single people don't have the option of staying home with a young child or the finances to enroll a child in daycare. Since older children attend school they have a schedule more compatible to that of a working parent. Sandra decided that she would adopt an older school-age girl. She looked forward to sharing her love of travel, theatre, and music with her daughter. She was ready to pursue her dream.

The following month Sandra was given a profile of six year old Lissette from the Western part of her state. Lissette had been in two foster homes, the last with a nurturing elderly woman. The woman wanted to remain in contact with Lissette but felt it was better that she has a younger parent. She had been born to a mother who had been using crack cocaine and she had gone through withdrawal during her first month of life. However, since that time she had done beautifully and now performed at the top of her class. Lissette had taken an interest in learning to play the piano. Sandra, an avid music enthusiast, read her profile and felt an instant connection. She called her social worker and exclaimed, "I think I've found my daughter!"

Some, like Sandra, approach adoption having had a serious illness such as cancer. Others may be dealing with chronic conditions and fear this may preclude them from becoming an adoptive parent.

Most agencies will request assurance from a doctor that no matter what your condition, you will be capable of meeting the demands of parenting.

Michael – 1975 (Adopted when he was 38)

I made a promise to God…

Michael, a 38 year old gay man had returned from a tour of duty in Vietnam.

"When I was in Nam, I made a promise to God. I had held too many orphaned children in my arms. I knew that if I got through the war, I was going to do something meaningful with my life. The many children I had seen orphaned or injured haunted me. A couple who were good friends of mine had just adopted an infant from the first baby lift. I was glued to the TV watching the children disembark from the cargo plane. I knew what I had to do."

Michael contacted the agency that his friends had worked with and told them of his desire to adopt a child. Things moved very quickly from that point.

"Within a matter of weeks, I was contacted with news of siblings, a boy, eight, and a girl, seven, who were coming on the next airlift. I said 'yes' immediately and barely had time to catch my breath before running out to buy furniture and clothes."

Fortunately, Michael's large Italian family, including two sisters and two brothers, were willing to chip in. Within days they had furnished a room for each child and Michael began to brush up on his Vietnamese.

"I was lucky to have a lot of family support and since my brothers and I had a contracting business, I had built my own house with enough room for a growing family. I thought about my extended family and realized how much I had to offer a child."

Despite how positive he felt about his home and the support he had to offer, Michael realized he was creating a very non-traditional family. As excited as he was, he worried that the children would be affected by being raised by a single male. He was especially concerned that his daughter would not have a female role model.

"When I voiced my concerns to my oldest sister, she said she would help out in any way she could. She had always wanted a daughter and said that any child of mine would be family and I could count on her for anything."

Several of his friends, particularly his army buddies from Vietnam, while admiring his compassion, felt as though he was taking on too much, and questioned his decision to adopt. Michael had seen many friends returning from the war who had succumbed to the devastating effects of alcoholism and depression. *There but for the grace of God*, thought Michael. He felt he had been spared for a reason.

Michael struggled with his sexuality. Although he had dated women in his twenties, before going to Vietnam, nothing serious had developed. After the arrival of his children, he had little time or inclination to date. In spite of this, several women seemed intent on pursuing a relationship with him. "The fact that I was unable to reciprocate these feelings, although I genuinely liked several of the women, made me question my own sexuality. I tried to get closer to one woman in particular, and finally decided to see a counselor to sort out my feelings. In the course of therapy, I looked back on my life and realized I had been attracted to the same sex since childhood but denied these feelings because of my upbringing and religious beliefs. Once I realized I was gay, a huge weight was lifted. Over the next few years, I *came out* to my family and friends and most were not surprised with my revelation. In fact my sister asked what took me so long."

Despite Michael's relief at acknowledging his identity as a gay man, his life did not change significantly. Like any parent, his life was filled with soccer practice and PTA meetings. Eventually Michael went on to adopt three more children.

Single gay men and lesbians will often face more obstacles when they seek to adopt. However, with determination and research they can find agencies that will be supportive. Since we began our work in 1984, we have seen an increase in the number of gay men and lesbians who adopt. Many support groups focusing on exploring options for gay and lesbian parenting are now available. Our work has been focused around creating support networks for non-traditional families. Each non-traditional family has its own unique needs. It is helpful for these families to connect with each other when going through the adoption process, and beyond that, while raising their children (*For a list of resources for singles as well as LGBT prospective and adoptive parents see appendix).*

Claire – 1996 (Adopted when she was 40)

Adding to my family…

"I went through a terrible depression after my divorce. I really wanted a large family but my husband, Bill, was resistant. We were married almost 10 years before Eva, my daughter, was born. After her birth, Bill became distant. It became clear to me that he really had no interest in raising our daughter and seemed to be jealous of the attention I was giving to her. My priority was my child and I began to resent Bill's detachment.

My family had always been my foundation. I was the middle child of three in a close Jewish family, and had fond memories of growing up with my siblings. My brother had no children and my sister's kids were grown. The fact that Eva would not have siblings or cousins close in age troubled me.

After a year of turmoil, Bill decided to move out of the house and I knew I couldn't depend on him for any kind of support, emotional or financial. After a trial separation, we decided to divorce."

Despite the lack of support from Bill, Claire received a great deal of support from her parents, who were doting grandparents, and her younger brother and older sister. She had an excellent job as an occupational therapist and was able to live a comfortable lifestyle. Always a wise investor, after her divorce Claire purchased a two-family house in an excellent school district. Thinking ahead, she envisioned she might one day rent the downstairs apartment to a tenant who could also provide childcare.

At age 40, Claire had a bright five year old, a close support network, and she was managing her life quite well. However, she had never anticipated raising a child on her own and always had hopes of having more children.

"From the time of my divorce, I focused entirely on raising my daughter. I'd begun to see a therapist and she was my lifeline during that time. She helped me to realize that I was a survivor. I was proud of how my daughter and I had bounced back after the divorce. One of the things I had shared with my therapist was the sadness I felt about the fact that I would probably never have a larger family."

One day, Eva had a play date with Hannah, a classmate of hers. Claire was surprised to learn that Hannah's mom, Amy, had adopted her from Romania as a single parent.

"Amy and I began talking and something inside of me clicked. I suddenly realized adoption was an option. I couldn't get the thought out of my mind and decided to talk about it with my therapist. Over the next several months I began to explore the idea of adoption further. It was during that time that Amy and I and Hannah and Eva grew closer."

The two mothers provided ongoing support for one another. Hannah would spend Friday nights with Claire and Eva while her mom took an exercise class and Eva would spend Sunday nights with Hannah and Amy so that Claire could join a book club. It worked well for both mothers and the girls enjoyed spending time together.

Claire became increasingly excited about the possibility of adoption. "I adored Hannah," said Claire, "and through her realized I could love a child who was not mine by birth. When I asked Eva how she would feel if I adopted a child, she was ecstatic and begged me to adopt a baby brother or sister for her. Her enthusiasm was all I needed to move forward." Claire wondered how an agency would view her – a divorced mother with a five year old child.

Her therapist wrote a letter of support stating that she felt Claire would be a good candidate as an adoptive parent, and that she had done a good job of raising her daughter through some difficult times.

Claire went to the same agency Amy had used. They had a program in Romania that accepted singles. The home study was completed in two months and Claire was overjoyed when three months later she received a photo of two year old Nadia. "Every night my five year old daughter kissed the picture of her new sister and placed it under her pillow."

Whether they have a biological child or an adopted child, many singles decide to add to their

31

family. This will inevitably be a major change for both parent and child. While the parent needs to make the final decision, allowing the child to voice their feelings about adding to the family will make for a smoother transition. While adding to the family can be an exciting and happy time, it can also bring up a range of feelings for both parent and child. The parent may worry about whether she will have enough time, energy and financial resources to support a growing family, and the child, while he may be looking forward to a sibling, may also experience feelings of displacement and jealousy. Consulting a therapist can provide the support needed for this period of adjustment.

Making a thoughtful decision…

These seven vignettes are based on true stories and are typical of the people we have seen in our clinical practice over the past 25 years. The vignettes are informed as well by the 77 participants who completed our survey. One thing stands out clearly: The decision to adopt was not made lightly. Each person made a thoughtful decision based on self-reflection and planning. Prospective single adoptive parents commonly struggle with many questions. These include:

- Is it fair to a child to be raised by a single person?
- How will I provide for my child(ren) emotionally and financially?
- How will this decision impact my life?

- What kind of child (gender, age, race, religion, ethnicity) could I best parent?
- Should I consider a child with special needs?
- Should I consider a sibling group?
- How would I feel about raising an adopted child?
- As a single parent, who would care for my child if I were to become disabled or die?
- Will I be able to balance my work schedule with the needs of a child?
- How will I develop a support network for my child and myself?
- How will I provide opposite sex role models for my child?
- If my child is of a different race or ethnicity, how will I provide experiences or role models to help him/her create a positive identity?

Our book will explore the many facets of the decision to adopt as a single person as well as the experiences of single adoptive parents raising their children. Most singles who adopt are strong, motivated, self-sufficient and compassionate individuals who are ready to embrace the challenges and joys of parenting.

CHAPTER TWO

The History of Single Parent Adoption

The past thirty years have shown a huge growth in single parent adoption. Sarah, Linda, Jill, Grace, Sandra, Michael and Claire found ways to become single adoptive parents and over the past decades our numbers have grown.

Although informal adoption by single women has always been present in our society, formal adoption by singles did not start to take place until the 1960s. One of the earliest efforts to place a significant number of children with single parents occurred in 1965 after the California State Department of Social Welfare revised its adoption regulation to permit single adults to become adoptive parents (Simon, R. J. and Howard Alstein, 1977. Feigelman, W. and Arnold R. Silverman, 1977: *Social Casework*). By 1967 the agency had placed 39 children in single parent homes. An evaluation of these first single parent adoptions found that, although a two-parent family was preferable, a stable single parent family was better for a child than the impermanence of foster care. In that same year, the Child Welfare League of America, which set the standards for over four hundred member agencies, announced that several agencies were ready to consider single parent placements for older African American or biracial children or for handicapped children who could not be placed in a two parent home (Klein, Carol, *Single Parent Experience,* 1973). This was an important shift in policy regarding single parent adoption. As the Los Angeles County Director of Adoptions stated, "To a child who may grow up without any family, the question of choice is irrelevant" (Klein, 1973, p. 92).

In 1970, Alfred Kadushin, one of the major researchers in the field of adoption, published an article, "Single Parent Adoption: An Overview and Some Relevant Research in the Social Service Review." In his conclusion he states that:

> The single-parent adoptive family is likely to be the kind of single-parent family which is least pathogenic. The inference is that while the two-parent nuclear family is the most familiar way to rear children it is not necessarily the only way and, indeed, for some children it may not be the best way. (Kadushin, 1970, p.271)

As a respected leader in the social work field, Kadushin's article held considerable influence. It was cited in most of the research that followed on single parent adoptions in the 1970s and 1980s. It also was particularly influential in stimulating single parent placements. In the child welfare arena Feigelman and Silverman conclude that their research supports the new and growing practice of single parent adoption. "Given the absence of a supportive spouse and their more limited economic resources, these positive findings suggest that single adoptive parents possess unusually high commitment to parenting" (1977, p. 425).

Sharon Doherty (1978) analyzed the adoption process as experienced by single women. Doherty found that a common practice was that the least "preferred" children were placed with the least "preferred" families. Even with mounting evidence that single mothers could be successful adoptive placements, and with gender roles becoming less rigid, most agencies still saw single adoption as a placement of last resort.

International adoptions by singles began to expand in the 1980s. Since that time there has been a steady increase of singles adopting from a wide array of countries. As noted below, while some countries have closed their adoption programs, others have opened new programs.

Increasingly singles have begun to look at domestic adoption. One option is the foster-adoption program where children are placed as foster children and if they become available for adoption, the foster parent is often given the opportunity to adopt the child. Another option is private adoption of infants. While in the past birthparents rarely chose a single person to raise their child, we have seen this trend change over time.

In the past thirty years we have seen a tremendous increase in the number of singles contemplating adoption and becoming adoptive parents. Single-parent adoption has filtered into our national consciousness. High-profile celebrities such as Diane

Keaton, Meg Ryan, Calista Flockhart and Paula Poundstone, and priests such as Father George Clements, as well as numerous others from all walks of life have adopted as single parents.

Whereas, single parent adoption may have previously been confined to a few urban areas, today the phenomenon has spread to include not only urban but also suburban and rural settings.

Whereas, social workers and educators predominated as single parents, today single parent adoption attracts people in a variety of professions and socioeconomic groups.

Whereas, thirty years ago children available to singles were almost exclusively older or had some type of mental, emotional, or physical special need, today the availability of children is greater, and includes healthy toddlers and infants. Whereas, gay men and lesbians had to hide their sexual orientation in the past, today, while adoption by gay men and lesbians is still not permitted in many countries, it is, at least theoretically, legal in all states in the US. In 2010, the state of Florida stopped enforcing its ban on adoption by gay men and lesbians (National Center for Lesbian Rights, 2010).

Single parent adoptions have increased in recent years due to a variety of reasons. These include:

1. A growing body of research documents the positive outcomes of placing children in single parent homes.
2. In April 1972, the National Association of Black Social Workers condemned trans-racial adoption

(Klein, 1973). While this increased the availability of black and biracial children for single black women, it significantly limited transracial adoption for Caucasian couples as well as singles. In 1994, the Multiethnic Placement Act (MEPA) was passed. This law prohibits a federally assisted agency from categorically denying the opportunity for any person to become an adoptive or foster parent solely on the basis of the race, color, or national origin of the adoptive parent or the child (Varon, *Adopting on Your Own*: *The Complete Guide to Adopting As a Single Parent,* 2000, p.151). The capacity of the adoptive parent to meet the child's needs based on the child's background can still be considered as one factor in the placement decision. This law, however, did significantly increase the practice of transracial adoption.

3. International adoption began to open up in the early '80s. While couples had begun adopting internationally in the '70s, things changed dramatically in the '80s when several countries, including India, Brazil, El Salvador, Peru, Honduras, Bolivia, Columbia and Paraguay, began to place children in single parent homes in the US. A major development occurred in the early '90s when both China and Russia opened their doors to allow single parent adoption. Unfortunately China has closed to singles and Russia was closed for a period of time. While some countries have closed others have opened. Several countries, including Liberia, Thailand, Kazakhstan, Bulgaria, Haiti, India and

Ethiopia are among those currently open to singles. During the three decades we have been working with single adoptive parents one thing that remains constant is that things change. Often without warning a program will shut its door to singles but invariably other avenues open up. Those singles who persist eventually do bring home their child.

CHAPTER THREE

Families Created by Single Parent Adoption

This book is based on feedback from single adoptive parents across the nation. We placed notices on many adoptive parent websites, and wrote to numerous agencies and support groups. We also talked to many past participants of our own decision-making groups. In all, we made contact with 77 parents who had adopted prior to 1996. We wanted to include parents who had gone through at least ten years of parenting and exclude new parents who may still be in the midst of a "honeymoon" period. We were also hoping to include parents whose children had gone through adolescence.

The parents represented here are, for the most part, Caucasian, heterosexual, and college educated. Of the 77 participants, 72 were Caucasian. The remaining five survey participants were Hispanic, African American, Native American and Asian. Ninety percent of the participants were heterosexual, 8% gay or lesbian, and 2% bisexual.

Many survey participants were members of our decision-making groups. They were largely middle class and reflected the communities we were working with. The majority were women, although four participants were male. Forty-nine percent had adopted one child and

41% adopted two. Only 4% had adopted three children and of the remaining 6%, two had adopted four children, one had adopted five, and one had adopted six children.

The age of the parent when adopting the first child ranged from 26 to 52, with 40 as the median age. The age of the parent when adopting additional children ranged from 30 to 57.

When did people choose to adopt?

Jill, a marketing director for many years, felt she was ready to start a family at 46. "I had done the 'career thing' and traveled. I wanted to be a parent and at that point in my life I was able to do so without feeling that I missed out on other things. I felt since I was older, I would be a better parent. I believe if I didn't have the life experience I had, the adoption could have been difficult. However, as I have aged, it's been harder to participate in physical activities and I often wish I had more energy. Also, I worry about the fact that, as an older single parent of one child, it will be hard for my daughter if anything happens to me. I'm all she has and I wouldn't want her to experience another loss."

Linda was 32 when she adopted her sons, Richie, five, and Jessie, three. She had always dreamed of being a mom and started the process as soon as she was able. "I wanted to have enough energy to keep up with young children. I really wasn't interested in finding a partner or having a biological child. So when I turned 32 I felt there was nothing stopping me except my finances. It was a struggle raising my boys on a limited income. I was constantly looking for ways to cut costs."

As Jill's and Linda's stories illustrate, there are many things to consider when making the decision to adopt. The concerns they raise were common to the prospective parents in our decision-making groups. Since the median age of first adopting was 40, in our experience we have found the decision to adopt is usually preceded by many years of questioning, soul-searching and information gathering. This is an important and necessary process and should not be short-circuited. Some singles contemplating adoption had hoped to find a partner with whom to parent and were disappointed when this didn't happen. Feelings of anger, resentment, depression and sadness may surface as singles witness friends or relatives marrying or finding partners while they remain single. Societal pressures and traditions often reinforce and magnify these feelings. While these emotions will vary in intensity from person to person, we feel it is important to acknowledge them and work them through. Adopting a child can bring much happiness and satisfaction to one's life, however a child cannot replace the longing for a partner. It is important to address the feelings that may arise from the absence of a partner before one embarks on the adoption process.

Many singles we spoke to felt adoption was a liberating and empowering life choice. Others however felt the loss of being able to have a biological child. We do not have statistics which document how many single adoptive parents experienced infertility before deciding to adopt, however, of those we contacted, the majority said adoption was their first choice in the process to becoming a parent. Since we began our work in 1984, societal attitudes towards women choosing to become pregnant without a partner have changed significantly. Even if adoption is a first choice, feelings of loss can still arise. As one woman explains, "I felt that in the absence of a committed relationship, adoption was right for me. If I had been married, while I might have adopted a child, it would not have been my first choice." So while some singles may have gone through difficult, expensive and time-consuming fertility treatments on their own, others may have chosen to adopt given the fact that they did not have a partner with whom to parent. In either case, feelings of anger and sadness may arise as normative stages of a grieving process. Our decision-making groups offered a safe place where people could express their feelings without being judged. Whether it's in a group, with an individual counselor or a trusted friend(s), it is helpful to have a place to share your feelings as you move through the adoption process.

While it's generally true that younger parents may have more energy and older parents more life experience, one's chronological age may be less important than whether one has matured and is emotionally ready to become a parent.

Who are the children?

The children in our survey, many of whom are now adults, come from 16 countries and seven states. There is a large group of adopted children from Latin America and India since many of the earliest single parent international adoptions took place from those countries.

The Latin American countries include Mexico, Ecuador, Colombia, Peru, Guatemala, El Salvador and Honduras. Other countries that are represented in our survey include Brazil, Haiti, Poland, Russia, Romania, China, Vietnam and Cambodia. Domestic adoptions include both same race and transracial adoptions, and include several states of origin. Many of the parents talked about the importance of raising their children in a diverse community and others discussed the challenges of being a minority family within a predominantly white community.

How old were the children when they were adopted?

Although there are often unknowns when adopting an infant, many believe that there is less risk involved as compared to adopting an older child. It is true that you have more control in some ways over the environment of your child if they are adopted in infancy. For example, there is more assurance that they will have good nutrition, appropriate medical care, and a safe and nurturing home. However, such things as the medical history of the birth parents, whether the child has an

45

underlying medical and/or developmental problem, and the temperament of the child may not be known.

Grace chose an open adoption of a newborn because raising a child from infancy was very important to her. "I was able to adopt my son when he was an infant and our bonding was immediate. I felt my son was a healthy, happy child with no damage from post-birth neglect or abuse."

Some chose to adopt an older child for a variety of reasons. Belinda, a nature photographer stated "I felt that an older child would have less opportunity to be adopted and I wanted to give a home to a child in need. I also felt that since I didn't have a partner, the demands of an infant would be too great for me as a single parent. I had an active lifestyle that I hoped an older child could more easily adapt to."

Sandra was 42 when she decided to adopt six year old Lissette. Sandra had survived cancer; that experience was her catalyst to acknowledging the importance of family and beginning the process of exploring adoption. Due to her demanding job and active lifestyle, Sandra felt she could best parent an older child. "Practically speaking, I didn't need daycare for my six year old daughter, and we still had time to bond before her adolescence."

Jessica, a second grade teacher, adopted a school-age child and two years later, a toddler. She believed she could have a greater impact on a child adopted at a younger age. Although both children, adopted internationally, suffered from the effects of poverty and the loss of their birth family and culture, their experiences were very different. It turned out that her older child had received early nurturing and was therefore more capable of bonding. Her younger child had been born in the midst of a civil war and spent his first two years in an overcrowded orphanage. While adopted at a younger age, the bonding process with her younger child proved more difficult.

The age at which a child is adopted is only one factor that may affect adjustment. At the time of adoption, the age of the children surveyed ranged from zero to age 14 for the first child. Almost half of the children adopted were less than a year old, and almost a quarter of the children were adopted between the ages of one and two. The remaining 25% of the children were adopted above the age of three.

Despite the joy of becoming a parent, whether you adopt an infant, a toddler, or an older child, there are bound to be challenges. For those who adopted younger children, feelings of isolation and limited time to socialize with peers, as well as sleep deprivation were often voiced. Older children, while usually more easily integrated into the life of a single working parent, will come with history which can place many demands on a single parent. We discuss these issues in later chapters.

Gender and adoption

Within our survey, girls were adopted twice as often as boys. One reason for this seems to lie in the fact that more women adopt and are frequently more comfortable raising a child of the same sex.

Jill stated, "I always wanted a daughter. I specifically requested a girl and that's one reason I chose China which only allowed same sex adoption for singles at that time. My father died when I was young and I was raised as an only child by my mother. I know very little about boys and would not have felt competent to raise a boy."

In addition, Jill felt like many adoptive moms, that it might be easier to raise a child of the same gender. "I felt I could share my personal experience of what it was like growing up as a woman. As I look back however I'm not sure how important this issue was to our relationship."

Many however, had no preference as to the gender of their child and several women actually preferred to raise a boy.

Lindsay, 37 and a stock broker, had always been a "tomboy" and preferred baseball over dolls and mechanics over make-up. Since she was able to state a preference, she chose to adopt a boy.

Gayle, an artist who "came out" as a lesbian at the age of 14 and decided to adopt at 40, stated, "The only thing I was sure of when I first began the adoption process, was that as long as I had a choice, I would adopt a girl. My life was surrounded with women and I had never considered adopting a boy. However, when my social worker presented me with the picture of two year old Danny, I fell in love. Now, twenty-five years later, I know I made the right decision. My son has been a joy to raise, and today I am a proud grandmother of twin boys and my son is a very devoted dad."

Some women questioned whether they could adequately provide male role models, and therefore decided to adopt girls. We believe that role models of the opposite sex are important for all children.

One lesbian mom talks about the importance of role models of both sexes. "As I, (and later my partner) and our kids are all female, we made consistent efforts to have good men (relatives, friends, teachers, babysitters) and excellent role models in our lives."

Jill commented, "Since my father had died, I was saddened by the fact that my uncle, who had no kids, initially disapproved when I adopted my daughter. Eventually though he developed a wonderful relationship with Kim. He dotes on her."

Gender issues

Carol, a tax accountant who adopted a son from Honduras felt he longed for a man in his life, particularly as adolescence approached. "My father died when my son was 12 and it was a tremendous loss. He used to take him fishing and to the ball game. I did things with him too, but it wasn't the same. He really missed having his Grandfather."

Linda felt strongly about providing positive male role models for her sons. "I tried to be diligent about providing positive males in their lives but it was difficult. We had to wait a couple of years but finally my sons were paired with two wonderful 'Big Brothers' through the *Big Brothers Big Sisters Association* and that made a huge difference in their lives."

People often ask how a child can grow up with a healthy attitude towards both sexes in a one-parent home. In most cases, single adoptive parents have given a lot of thought about how to incorporate role models of the opposite sex into their family. We never encountered a single adoptive parent who felt this was simply not an issue. Whether it's through one's immediate family and friends, Big Brothers Big Sisters type organizations, church or synagogue, daycare or sitters, school or pre-school, singles work to ensure that their children are exposed to positive and caring people of both sexes.

Religion

The religious views of the adoptive parents in our survey range greatly and include Jewish, Catholic, Unitarian, Protestant, as well as agnostic and atheist. The religion of the adoptive parent often determined the religion of the child. This was clearly the case for children adopted at a younger age. The outcomes varied for those who were adopted when they were older and

50

had been exposed to a different religious faith prior to their adoption. Some older children felt they wanted to continue the religious practices they were accustomed to. Whereas others were open to taking on the religion of their adoptive family.

Many adoptive parents were committed to their religion and found their church or synagogue a place of refuge, support, and social stimulation.

Linda stated; "I get tremendous support from my faith, it sets the values and morals for everything. When I adopted the boys they had been accustomed to attending mass with their foster parent. So the transition to attending my church was easy."

One Jewish mother of a Chinese daughter noted that her daughter "goes to Hebrew School and takes Chinese lessons. It's all part of who she is."

Another mom talked about her son's Bar Mitzvah. "My son arrived from Brazil at the age of nine; he had been raised by nuns and had no idea about Judaism. After attending his cousin's Bar Mitzvah, he decided he wanted to complete his Bar Mitzvah. When the celebration was complete, he whispered to me, 'Can I be a Christian again?' I responded, 'That's fine. You are whoever you need to be.'"

For many adopted children the desire to assimilate is strong and they readily accept the religion of their adoptive parent; however, there can be a conflict if the child is reluctant to do so. It is important for a parent to broaden their perspectives to embrace a child's past and religion may be an important part of this. The Jewish mom whose son was raised as a Catholic found a Catholic friend who was willing to take her child to Mass.

Single parent adoptions gain credibility

While many adoption programs favor two-parent families, it is our belief that single parents can offer a strong, nurturing and stable environment in which to raise children. In fact, given the high rate of divorce, many children who were adopted by a couple who subsequently divorce, will experience the challenges of both adoption and divorce. This book will illustrate that with support, resources, education, and careful planning, a single parent family should be considered as a positive placement for children.

Although there are many challenges to adopting as a single parent, we believe singles bring unique strengths and insight to the parenting experience. In some cases, social workers see singles as the "placement of choice" for children who may require the focused attention of one parent. Particularly for children who have had difficulty adjusting in a two-parent home, a single parent home can be a preferred placement.

We have learned from our work and the responses to our surveys that single people, for the most part, do not undertake parenthood lightly. On the contrary, it is our experience that they often spend a great deal of time researching the pros and cons of parenting on their own, talking to other adoptive and single parents, gathering information and soul-searching before they embark on adoption.

Many single adoptive parents are older when they decide to adopt. The average age in our survey was 40. Singles who adopt are often more mature when they come to the parenting experience. As one mother of two boys said: "I no longer sweat the small stuff, becoming a parent set my priorities straight."

Because single adoptive parents know from the start that they are embarking on parenthood on their own, they usually make a concerted effort to create a network to support themselves and their child(ren). They know they can't "do it alone" when it comes to the emotional part of parenting. They need support and they are adept at finding it. We have often seen that couples who divorce and find themselves dealing with solo parenting may have less support than singles who have planned for this role.

Although single parenthood by choice is becoming more prevalent and widely accepted, it is sometimes seen as a nontraditional lifestyle. Singles who decide to raise a child on their own may experience reactions of others which are less than favorable. These reactions can leave them feeling marginalized or judged based solely on their decision to parent on their own.

As we in the adoption community know, adopted children (despite the increase in adoption and acceptance of adoption in our culture) often struggle with feelings of being different. Because many single adoptive parents have also experienced feelings of being different in our society, single adoptive parents are often uniquely qualified to help adopted children with their own identity struggles. This is not to equate the emotional and psychological issues of single adoptive parenting with that of being adopted. It is rather, to recognize that in both cases individuals can experience themselves as being outside of mainstream society which can create a bond between them.

A single mother of three said: "There are some things we don't have in our family… like we don't have a Dad… but rather than focus on that, I look at all we do have – a wonderful family, a great community with lots of different kinds of families, and a strong support network."

CHAPTER FOUR

From Single Person to Single Parent: Making the Decision

Much of our work has been focused on the decision to adopt. We feel it is important to make this decision with utmost care as it will have far reaching effects on your life, and should you choose to adopt, on the life of your child. The disruption of an adoption is traumatic for everyone involved.

We will give the reader a first-hand account of the decision making process through the eyes of singles who have made this decision. Starting with their motivations to adopt as single parents, we will follow their decision-making processes, identifying common concerns and obstacles.

<u>Reasons to adopt as a single person</u>

Why do single people decide to adopt? What motivates them? How do they make this decision that will change their lives forever?

For many people, turning 40 is a time of coming to terms with the choice of becoming a parent – or not. "I was approaching 40," said Ruth, a government worker, "and had no prospects of marriage, and I wanted a child. I didn't want the pregnancy experience as much as I wanted the parenting experience. At about the same time, I heard that single women could adopt baby girls from China and I never looked back."

Many women felt that turning 40 represented the end of their fertility and was the time to seriously consider whether or not they would ever become pregnant.

Sarah echoed the sentiments of many single women: "After my relationship with Brad ended, it looked as if I wasn't going to find 'prince charming' and become a mother by biological means. So I decided to do it on my own through adoption. I had just turned 40. I didn't feel strongly that I needed to have biological children, particularly since I wasn't in a relationship, and I felt competent to raise children on my own. I had a well-established career as a teacher and earned a good salary. I owned a home. I thought, 'Other women have done this before me, and I can do it too.'"

In the early '80s when we (The Adoption Network) started running decision-making groups for singles exploring adoption, there were few people who had chosen this path to parenthood. People in our workshops were hungry to see and hear others who were exploring the same decision. One woman told us our workshop was the first place she had been where she felt people didn't look at her like she "had two heads" when she told them she was single and wanted to adopt. Another woman said our workshop was the first place she felt as if her desire to adopt on her own was not pathologized.

While 44% of our survey participants decided to adopt for the first time between the ages of 39 and 43, there were some single people who had adopted much earlier and seemed to always know they wanted to adopt. While the youngest survey participant was 26 at the time he adopted; there were three people who adopted for the first time at age 49.

A social worker, Laura, was 16 in the 1960s when she read a newspaper article about a single woman who had adopted and decided she'd like to do the same thing one day. Following her mother's death during her junior year of college, Laura's longing for family was intensified. The thought of adoption had always been on her mind. When she found she was not in a relationship at the age of 30, she decided to pursue her lifelong dream. "I always wanted to be a mother – more than I wanted to be a wife," she wrote. Laura adopted her first child when she was 33.

Leslie saw a program on TV about the plight of children in Vietnam who had been fathered by African American servicemen, and while she herself didn't adopt from Vietnam, she went on to adopt biracial children from the U.S. when she was 34.

Kris, an administrative social worker said: "I had always wanted and expected to have children. In my mid-thirties with no potential partner, I decided to pursue parenthood – something more within my control than finding a man. I chose to adopt thinking there was a child who needed a parent as much as I needed a child.

Besides, I couldn't see myself enduring a solo pregnancy or being single and pregnant at my job."

While there were few men who adopted, the majority of those we spoke with made the decision to adopt before the age of 40. Michael, who had served in Vietnam, saw many children who were orphaned. He made a promise to God that if he returned from the war, he would try to adopt children. He was 38 when he adopted the first two of his five children.

For them and others, forty was not the magic age at which they began to consider parenting on their own. They decided to adopt in their twenties or thirties. Forty per cent of the people we spoke to decided to adopt before the age of forty, and of those, 23% decided to adopt before 35 and 1% before 30.

Linda adopted her two boys when she was 32. Many singles we spoke with who worked with children, particularly those in the adoption field, were open to adopting at an early age. They had seen first-hand the children who needed parents, and they were familiar with families formed through adoption.

Linda said: "I was not married. I adopted two kids that our agency could not find homes for. I just feel so blessed that these are the two boys God chose for me."

Other singles, while not working directly with a child welfare agency, had made one or more personal contacts that prompted them to consider adopting. Nina, a bookstore owner who adopted at 38, said: "I always thought I would have biological and adopted children. I was always interested in adoption. I even worked in an orphanage right after high school. When my best friend Jo Ann adopted her daughter from Colombia, I began looking into adoption." Two years later, Nina traveled to Colombia to meet and adopt her six year old daughter, Ana.

Andy, a social worker who had volunteered with children, was only 26 when he adopted his first child, a thirteen year old Caucasian boy who was living at a residential treatment center. He went on to adopt two more sons, eight year old biracial twins.

Although some singles we spoke with did adopt before 40, the majority (52%) were in their 40s and only two were in their 50s when they first adopted. It is important to note that the people who participated in our research adopted primarily in the 1980s. While most of the people we spoke with adopted in their 40s, increasingly people are exploring adoption at both younger and older ages.

Some singles were raising a birth child when they made the decision to adopt. Usually, they were widowed or divorced. They chose to adopt because they wanted to add to their family and they often said they wanted siblings for their child. Claire said: "I had one birth child – I wanted more. I wanted to be a mother. I liked being a mother. I didn't want my child to grow up alone."

Many single women did not know their fertility status and had never attempted to become pregnant. Of the singles we spoke to, the majority, 75%, didn't attempt to become pregnant before deciding to adopt, and 25% didn't even consider having a biological child. Our survey participants adopted their children in the '70s, '80s and early '90s and at the time they felt it was more socially acceptable to adopt rather than become pregnant on their own. Sarah felt that as a teacher, she would not be comfortable going through a pregnancy on her own: "I'm single and for me adoption was the only way I would consider becoming a mother." Society's view of single women choosing to become pregnant has changed since our survey participants adopted.

Some single women were not comfortable giving birth for other reasons. Others – both men and women – felt that they would rather provide a home for a child who needed one rather than bring a child into the world. As Pam, a devout Catholic who adopted at 33, said: "My religion cannot sanction a pregnancy outside of a marriage. I felt adoption was the only option I had as a single person." Donna, a physician's assistant who adopted at 36, said: "It felt selfish to bring another child into the world when there were so many already that needed homes."

Others, like Lorna, a financial analyst who adopted at 41, felt that in the absence of a committed, loving relationship, having a biological child was less of a priority. She felt being pregnant as a single woman would be a lonely experience.

While some singles did not choose to explore their fertility status, other women assumed they could become pregnant but chose to adopt.

In the '80s when many single people began adopting, reproductive technologies were not as sophisticated or available as they are today, and many single women in their 40s felt pregnancy was no longer possible for them. Some attempted to become pregnant and when this path didn't work out, chose to adopt.

Many single women who tried and were unable to get pregnant did not want to go through fertility treatments on their own. For others, the expense of such treatments was prohibitive.

For some, transitioning to adoption seemed to occur soon after they found out they were unable to conceive. They moved from considering pregnancy to pursuing adoption with relative ease. Gwen, a clinical psychologist, adopted six month old Joseph from Mexico when she was 41. She said: "I knew I wanted a child although I was infertile. The moment I found out I couldn't conceive, I started the adoption process."

Grace, who adopted her infant son when she was 36 stated: "Trying to get pregnant and going through infertility treatments wasn't working. But boy am I glad because I feel my son was the child I was meant to have."

For Grace and many others, the process of moving from trying to conceive to choosing adoption could be long and arduous. Karen, a hospital administrator, experienced four miscarriages. "I tried donor insemination for many years and also three rounds of IVF. After many miscarriages I set myself a deadline and decided to go forward with adoption at 42."

Betsy said that by the time she adopted at 42, she had dealt with infertility for twelve years. She felt she had grieved the loss of a birth child and was ready to move on to form a family through adoption. For Grace and Betsy and many others, these attempts to conceive were costly and took a huge emotional and physical toll. "My body and my bank account were exhausted!" exclaimed Betsy, at one of our group sessions.

Sometimes other medical conditions resulted in infertility. Sheila, a high school math teacher, had cancer when she was 22 and had a complete hysterectomy. Eventually, at the age of 35, once she had a clean bill of health for five years, she went on to adopt Alma and Estela, sisters from El Salvador.

There were many reasons why people chose adoption as a way to start a family. But in response to our question, "Why did you choose to adopt?" singles overwhelmingly spoke about their burning desire to create a family, and their love of children, as the primary reasons for adopting. The following quotes illustrate this:

- "I wanted to be a parent with or without a partner."
- "My life was going well but I longed to share it with children."

- "I wanted a child in my life to share each day."
- "I knew I needed children in my life…to fully experience motherhood. I was especially close to my godchildren but needed the experience of raising a child and sharing my life with a child to make my life more meaningful."
- "I loved children and I wanted the experience of raising and nurturing a child."

The concept of family was often an important factor for singles that chose to adopt. Many told us that just because they had never married, they saw no reason to give up the nurturing and life-expanding experience of having a family.

Transition to single adoptive parent

In the decision-making groups that we ran (at The Adoption Network), we saw more than one woman who arrived at the group straight from seeing her doctor for her insemination. To be pursuing adoption and a pregnancy at the same time can clearly lead to conflicting emotions. It is recommended that anyone who has tried and been unable to conceive give herself a period of time to mourn the loss of a biological child before moving on to adoption.

Sometimes, the end of a long-term relationship was the precipitating event to adopting. This may cause a single person to reevaluate her life journey and realize how important parenting is – with or without a partner. Singles who went on to adopt said they couldn't imagine going through life without having a child, and the end of a relationship often forced them to realize that their dream of marriage and family would not unfold exactly as planned. This prompted them to look at other ways of realizing their dream of parenthood. As Sarah said: "My long-term relationship was clearly going nowhere and I desperately wanted to be a parent. I was six years older than my partner, and I hit 40 when he was just 34 – and he was very immature. I didn't obsess about getting pregnant; I always felt that adoption was a wonderful way to have a child, and when I decided to turn to plan B, i.e., ending the relationship and embarking on parenting on my own, adoption was clearly the best route for me."

Tamara, a pharmacist who adopted at 42, spoke poignantly of losing hope of finding a partner and building a family. "I arrived at a point where I realized I would need to take action on my own if I were ever going to have the family I wanted. Whether I met someone or not, I wasn't willing to wait any longer to become a parent."

Cynthia, a social worker who adopted at 36, said: "I realized that dream of a family I had grown up believing in was not going to happen for me. It took some time to let that dream go and move on to building my own dream."

For people who are used to the freedom of a single lifestyle, adopting a child is a radical change. Suddenly, one can't go out to meet a friend on the spur of the moment. Myra, an interior designer spoke of how she adopted an infant when she was 37 and brought him home in the midst of a huge snowstorm. Sunday morning, after his arrival, she got ready to go out and get the Sunday paper a few blocks away. Suddenly, she stopped and realized that not only did she need to bundle up her son and get him into his stroller; she also needed to figure a way to get his stroller through mounds of snow. It was at that moment when she realized, "there are a lot of things I hadn't thought of."

One of the issues important to address during this period of transition is the loss of freedom. Denny, a project manager, adopted eight month old Carla from Guatemala when she was 38. Denny expressed the fear of never being able to spend a moment without being concerned about her infant daughter. "Even when I'm at work, I'm thinking of Carla. Her needs come first. I truly have no time to think of my own needs as mothering seems to be an around the clock commitment! As much as I love being a mom, I could really use a break once in a while."

Whether you choose to adopt or choose to remain childless there are adjustments involved. If the choice is to adopt, the more spontaneous single lifestyle is lost. When you become a single parent, control of your schedule changes dramatically. But if the choice is to remain childless, the experience of raising a child is lost.

Advice from single adoptive parents

Linda has strong feelings about the decision to adopt. "First of all, you have to know that you pass the test that applies to all potential adoptive parents: you have to know that you can love an adopted child as you would love a biological child. Also, you have to be absolutely clear in your desire for children. If you aren't sure that you want children you will have difficulty getting through everything that parenting throws at you. These issues have to be settled in your mind, so that you can move forward to the challenges of parenting. Second, you have to have a certain level of confidence that you can do this alone. You have to believe that you make enough money, are organized enough, and are sufficiently emotionally sound to cope. Just because your home study states that you are fit to be a parent, doesn't mean it will be easy. You will likely have to come to terms with being single for much of your adult life. I find lots of single adoptive moms think they will meet the love of their lives after they adopt. It happens on occasion, like for Angelina Jolie, but seems to be a challenge for most. Third, you have to have a certain tolerance for ambiguity and unanswered questions. Lots of the accomplished women I know tend to analyze things to death - and the unknown background of many of our adopted children doesn't allow for that. You are setting out on a road that opens you to many risks, most of them unpredictable at this point. Fourth, you have to be as persistent as the day is long. Simply completing an adoption takes an unbelievable amount of persistence, and parenting takes even more. Single parent adoption is not for the faint-hearted."

Jill, speaking of the decision to adopt advises, "Stop being so independent. Find other single adoptive parents and be as organized as possible. You are your own advocate in the process. Don't let anyone make you feel inferior because you are single! You are a perfectly suitable parent. When all else fails - keep your sense of humor!"

Sarah, who adopted Graciela from El Salvador, advises not to adopt a child out of a desire to rescue a child (or yourself) but out of a desire to share your life with a child. She offers her thoughts: "Be clear on why you want to adopt on your own and assess how you would do it. Assess what type of support system you have to make it work and consider what types of changes you might make to accommodate a child."

Summary

Some singles knew early in their lives that they wanted to be parents, with or without a partner. Very often, however, there were life-changing events that led them to choose the path of adoption. That event may have been reaching an age that they deemed a cut off point for becoming a parent; the choice to adopt may have begun when a relationship ended or when there was no partner in view; or it may have come after a history of infertility.

If you have any doubts about adopting as a single person, think about what your life would be like in ten years. At that stage in your life do you want to be a mother of a young child or teen? If there were no children in your life in ten years would you feel regret or would those energies you would have put into adopting a child be channeled into new pursuits?

Regardless of the path taken, support should be a vital component in making the decision to adopt as a single parent. Over the past two decades, the number of singles adopting has increased dramatically. Although groups such as the ones we ran in the '80s can be helpful, it is now much easier for people to find other singles who are either exploring adoption or have already adopted. Even those in remote areas who might not have had access to support in the past, now have access to online support groups. (see Appendix for a list of resources) Realizing that one can choose to adopt is often empowering. Only a few decades ago this option was not available to singles who longed for a family. Many of those we interviewed felt liberated in knowing that adoption was something they could choose to do on their own.

CHAPTER FIVE

Friends, Family and Support Networks

The decision to adopt as a single parent will change not only your life, but will significantly affect the lives of close friends and family. For many, this may be the first time the family has had an adopted person and perhaps a person of color as a member. Friends who have depended on you for vacations and social events will be faced with the reality that vacations will now be child centered, and as a single parent your priorities will be shifted. New relationships are created. Your siblings will become aunts and uncles and your parents will become grandparents. This phenomenon represents a shift in the most primary relationships in the adoptive parent's life and often precipitates stressors and unexpected challenges and joys.

A change in relationships

Most single adoptive parents did not view this change as a loss, but rather a transition to accommodate their new identity.

The importance of a support network resonated as the one most important variable in the lives of these single adoptive families. As a single adoptive parent, priorities will change to accommodate the needs of your new family.

After adopting, Sandra continued her work at the university. She was fortunate to have on-site afterschool care for her six year old daughter Lissette. She went through major changes when Lissette came into her life. "I changed my circle of friends to include many single parents. Some of my friends became former friends when they criticized my decision to raise a child on my own."

Jill was able to take a three-month leave from her job as Director of Marketing. Then to Jill's surprise, her aunt who had never had children, offered to care of Kim, her seven month old daughter. Jill hesitated at first, remembering her uncle's negative response to her decision to adopt. However, once Kim arrived home, her uncle changed his outlook and became protective and adoring of his new grand-niece.

Jill's circle of friends widened with the adoption of her daughter. She, like many other single adoptive parents sought out other families like her own. "After I adopted Kim, my social life involved getting together with other single moms with daughters from China."

Sarah adopted her eight month old daughter, Graciela from El Salvador. Like Jill, her child's ethnicity played a role in the development of her social circle. "My social life largely overlapped with those of other single parent families with kids from Central America. My social circles changed to reflect my role as a parent. Because most of my friends and colleagues were childless, we had less in common and our schedules rarely coincided."

70

In both Jill's and Sarah's cases, they sought out a support network of other single adoptive families. They arranged play groups and individual play dates. This helped normalize their existence as nontraditional families and these relationships grew stronger over the years.

Michael had adopted two children from Vietnam. His older sister Mary, a retired postal worker with grown children, took great interest in the children and picked them up from school every day and stayed with them until Michael was through with his workday. The children saw Mary as a mother figure and blossomed with the nurturing from both, Mary and Michael, as well as other members of his family. Michael, encouraged by the generous support of his family, went on over the next few years to adopt three biracial children, adding to his "rainbow family." "Being single," said Michael, "doesn't mean you have to go it alone. It helps to have a very large, and actively involved support group including parents, siblings, friends, social workers, teachers, and special education advocates. Think of it as an army with you being the commander-in-chief. And never think your child is deprived just because he or she doesn't have two parents. It's a sense of family and belonging that's important…. whatever form that family may take."

Living in a diverse community

Adopted children often express the feeling of being "different". Children of a different race or ethnicity than their parents have an additional challenge to overcome. Therefore, multiracial families frequently seek diverse communities. The phenomenon of wanting to "fit in" and assimilate peaks during adolescence, a time when the search for identity is paramount. Having a peer group to identify with becomes a primary issue in the life of most teenagers. Therefore, finding a community with other adopted children as well as other single parents can offer a sense of community and belonging. Living within a community of other single, adoptive, and multi-cultural multi-racial families helps "normalize" the existence of the single adoptive family.

Helen, an art therapist who became the mother of two boys from El Salvador, ages three and four when she was 39, felt it was a priority to live in an urban setting. "I chose to live in a liberal, diverse community where I felt my boys would fit in. For me and the boys, that factor took precedence over the trade-offs of a backyard and a white picket fence. I chose a community that had enough diversity so my children would not stand out – I always checked the mall and the composition of schools to make sure there was variety and a commitment to diversity."

Jo, a high school gym teacher who adopted at 46, chose her community given the diversity and special education support for her learning-disabled son. "Juan's needs were identified early and he has been receiving

72

excellent support and services in the public schools since he was two. It has made a big difference in our lives. My son has the opportunity of a good education and we live in a diverse community where there are other Hispanic children."

Some who lived where there was limited diversity looked elsewhere for diversity. The majority of those parents sought support within the adoption community, often traveling many miles to maintain those connections.

Karen adopted three year old Daniel from India. They lived in a white suburb outside of Hartford. Many weekends Daniel and Karen would drive 90 miles to Hartford to connect with other adopted families with children from other countries. Karen felt committed to expose Daniel to other adoptive families, many of whom had children from other countries.

As a single parent, the freedom of your old lifestyle will be altered significantly. Many of the single parents interviewed reported the importance of having supportive relatives to share parenting with. However, there were often trade-offs regarding the lack of cultural diversity in many neighborhoods where supportive family members were located.

Michael was able to maintain his full time employment in his family business as a contractor with his brothers because his parents and older sister were very involved in the day-to-day lives of his children. "We lived in the same neighborhood as my parents and sister, which was great. The downside was that my Asian and bi-racial children grew up in a primarily white community. On the positive side I knew my family was there for my kids and was close at hand if an emergency arose. They were there when they came home from school and cared about how their day went, made sure they had a snack and that the homework was completed. When I came home at night, I could enjoy my children without worrying about homework or preparing dinner. My children have fond memories of this time in their lives."

At 41, Stephanie, a literacy teacher, adopted her seven month old African American daughter. She felt it was important for her daughter to grow up within a diverse community and have role models to reflect her race and culture. "We lived in New York City until my daughter was in first grade. At that point, we moved closer to my sister and her kids to a mostly white suburb of New Jersey. I loved living near family, but felt the loss of a diverse community and access to other multiracial families. That issue took on greater importance as adolescence and self-image issues were emerging."

Support networks

Single adoptive parents often speak about the challenges of their changing relationships with friends and family. When one chooses to adopt their activities often shift to include other adoptive and especially single parents, and these newfound communities can add much to their lives. However, as many single adoptive parents come to rely on and socialize with those sharing their experience of parenting, their other relationships can change and become more distant.

Maddie, a paralegal and the mother of two girls, speaks of not fitting in with the married mothers of her children's friends, yet losing some of her single friends after she adopted. Finding the right kind of support is critical to the functioning of the family. While some friendships may fall by the wayside, single adoptive parents often work very hard to establish and maintain a supportive network for themselves and their children.

Alice, a young social service caseworker, adopted her five year old daughter when she was 26 and working in Washington. "It is essential that you have a support system. I had one when I adopted, but once I was promoted at work, I had to move across the state where I knew no one. There was no family or close friends that I could depend on and more importantly trust to take care of my daughter for a few hours or for a few days when I traveled for work. I realized I needed to go out and create a support system, but after working all day and coming home to family needs, my energy was often drained at the end of the day."

Even parents who had support from friends and family often felt periods of being alone. Paula, a magazine editor who became a mother at 44 to an eight year old African American son had a close support network. Even so, she felt single parent adoption created unique challenges. "I have been lucky enough to have family and friends to vent and share the good, the bad and the ugly with me. However, those folks are not around in the middle of the night or after bedtime when I have had to cope with situations or just worry by myself."

Grace felt the greatest challenge came from knowing that you are emotionally, financially, physically, and in every other way, responsible for another human being. She said, "It is amazing and also challenging, and sometimes frightening to know I am *it*. I can't always depend on friends and family."

Lois, an administrative assistant, who adopted her children as a single parent and then married, offers another opinion. "The marriage was difficult and at times I felt like a single parent with an additional child, my husband. When I think of that, I think that sometimes being a single parent has advantages over being married. When a divorce takes place, it represents another loss for the child. In a single parent household, the possibility of a divorce does not exist."

Michael offers this advice: "Support, support, support! It truly does take a village to raise a child, and going it alone as a single person makes the support of friends, family, church and other social groups critical. Learn to ask for help. Have a list of friends who can take your child for a while when you are at your wits' end. Don't lean on one person too much or you'll burn that person out! Join a support group. Ask for help. Being a single parent requires that we network, barter, and borrow."

Linda acknowledges the struggles of single parent adoption, "Most of the control over your life that you might think you have will be gone. Your children's needs become the priority, and this will affect your future decisions. In addition, any decisions they make can impact your life in a positive or negative way for years to come." As far as adopting as a single parent versus two parents is concerned, it is critical to have a support system of friends or family, specifically those who are connected to adoption as well as your child's cultural/ethnic background. Children adopted by single parents face many of the same issues as birth children who grow up with only one parent. But in addition, for the adopted child, there may be issues surrounding the adoption, i.e. loss of birth families and their lives prior to adoption. Having one parent may be an issue for some adopted children and not for others. Many of the adoptees of single parents we spoke with felt that adoption was a greater issue than the issue of being raised in a single parent home (See Chapter 9).

Jill recalls the positive experience of finding a support group while raising her child. "It was so much fun! We had very dear friends, also single women with adopted children, with whom we shared most weekends! The children developed relationships like cousins, and it gave the adults an immediate support network. The children became comfortable sleeping over at each other's homes and as a result, the adults had a free evening, knowing the children were well cared for and happy. These relationships with other single adoptive families helped normalize our experience and provided heartfelt and knowledgeable support. Today, thirty years after adopting our children, we still share deep friendships."

Many single adoptive parents noted the importance of support particularly around the teen years. One mom advises, "Do not underestimate the teen years. They are especially trying. I needed the support of others who were going through the same thing."

As the sole provider for their families, single adoptive parents may worry about their own health and what might happen if they become ill or die. Since many singles are older when they decide to adopt, it is not surprising that a number of people encountered their own health issues before or after adopting.

Brenda, a director of IT and communications, was 42 when she adopted a 15 month old girl. Diagnosed with breast cancer a year after her daughter arrived, she found it difficult to face her health problems alone. "I have had to learn to rely on others for help," she said, "and to plan for the future - facing the possibility that I may not live to see my daughter grow up. That was very frightening to me. As a result, I decided to move closer to my family."

Even without special health issues, the normal aging process can be an ongoing challenge for singles raising children alone. "Aging has been challenging because I adopted an infant in my mid-forties," said Jill, "I would definitely do it again, but if I could choose, I'd do it at a much younger point in my life."

Jenny, a lesbian, felt isolated in her community until she joined her church. "I lived in the suburbs, a middle class area and was searching for a support network which could welcome my son and me. So I joined my church because of its diversity and their welcoming of gay men and lesbians. The friends I made there made all the difference. In fact I actually met a woman at the church who was a single parent of twin boys, close in age to my son. We've been spending lots of time together and thinking about combining our households."

Charlotte, a financial planner, sought a different kind of support from a religious community. "Our neighborhood is diverse ethnically, but I don't know of any other adoptive families in the area. There are however, other adoptive parents that attend our synagogue, and that community has been immensely important to us. My daughter, adopted from China, got a lot of support for her Bat Mitzvah. Some of our best friends and greatest support were found at the synagogue."

Dating and beyond

Of the 77 people who responded to our survey, 65% were single, 16% were divorced, 13% were married (they were single at the time of their adoption) and 6% were living with a partner. They stated that at the time of their first adoption, 42% were not interested in dating, 35% were dating casually, and 23% were in a relationship that had lasted for more than six months.

Many years after adopting two year old Nadia from Romania, Claire became interested in dating. At that time her biological daughter, Eva, was approaching her teen years and Nadia was nine. Claire had an occasional date but felt dating was too great a challenge while raising her children. "Parenting was a full time job. I had no time to date. I was lucky if I got to see close friends. I tried casual dating through a service but had no luck and felt trying to date was a hassle. By the time I had arranged for a sitter and calmed the kids down, I just needed to chill out and spend time by myself. I was quite sure I wasn't ready to meet the demands of the dating world."

Dating was also a challenge for Diane, a freelance writer, who at 36 adopted seven year old Kristen. Kristen had been in several foster homes prior to living with Diane. Although she eventually married when Kristen became an adult, dating while Diane was raising her daughter proved difficult. "In the early years, my daughter was very critical of the men I dated. Dating didn't feel like a priority. I also felt my daughter needed me and I didn't want a relationship to take time away from her. She had experienced abandonment and had a tough time whenever I went out. Once my daughter was on her own, I felt I finally had the freedom to explore a social life. I met John at my high school reunion and we married the following year."

Sandra viewed her transition to motherhood as a trade-off. "If by social life you are referring to dating, the adoption of Lissette limited the time I could give to meeting new people. But in other ways I had more social opportunities as a parent to get together with other families. I met some really lovely people at Lissette's school and there was another network of folks we met through church. My life felt pretty complete. Fortunately I was able to arrange a time for my best friend to come over once a week and spend the evening with my daughter. This gave me some consistent free time and my daughter an opportunity to bond with another adult."

Jill agrees. "I did loads of child-centered activities with my daughter which I totally loved and I didn't feel deprived. I still went out with friends to movies and dinners but I didn't date. I waited a long time to be a mom so my daughter was my priority."

Marge, an event planner for a large hotel chain, adopted her infant son from Paraguay at 40. "It became more difficult to have my own social life as my son got older and developed his own social life. It was easier when he was little. At some point, my weekends centered around football games, school dances and chauffeuring him and his buddies around.

Linda was 32 when she adopted her sons. At the time, she had little interest in dating. "The last man I dated," she said "didn't want children. When I weighed the choice of being in a relationship versus becoming a mother, it was clear what my priority was."

Claire spoke of the freedom of adopting without a husband. She had been married and had one biological daughter. Later, she went on to adopt as a single parent. When she described her husband and marriage she stated: "Married at 30, divorced at 35. I was very resentful of the burden of household and parenting which was 90-10 instead of 50-50. My husband seemed to be another child who would never develop into a full-fledged adult. Adopting as a single parent was liberating!"

Betty was 32 when she adopted her nine year old son from Brazil. Dating had always been important to Betty and she felt, as a single parent, she would be able to attract a partner who shared her beliefs about adoption. Her son however, had a very different view.

"My son was quite jealous of any male attention I received and acted out whenever a male visitor came to the house. He had been abandoned by one mother and was not about to risk losing another. My daughter, adopted two years after my son, had a difficult time with a long-term boyfriend. I had to constantly juggle my schedule to avoid having my boyfriend and my daughter in the same setting. At some point I realized anyone in my life would have to accept my children or I would need to keep my dating life quite separate from them. This certainly narrowed down an already small number of eligible males who might be of interest to me and me to them.

"Once the kids became adults, I could finally pursue relationships without impacting my children. Today they understand and support my desire for a relationship and are my greatest advocates. It's been a long wait!"

Lydia, a physical therapist who adopted six year old Gerry from Bolivia at 40, explains: "Partners do not have the same interest in your child that you do. Sometimes time spent with a romantic partner meant time away from my son. Sometimes I spent time with both together and often I was exhausted trying to satisfy everyone's needs. It can get pretty complicated. There were times when Gerry would bond with a romantic partner of mine, only to suffer another loss at the end of our relationship. After a time, I decided to keep my social life separate from my life as a parent."

"It was a real challenge," says Sarah. "My daughter, although adopted as an infant, has always been hyper-aware of anything that could be construed as 'dating' a man and reacts with concern about being displaced (from my bed, from my attention). She doesn't mind when I spend time with my friends." Sarah decided not to pursue romantic relationships that might present problems with her daughter. "I decided to give up dating until my daughter is older. It's really kind of freeing!"

Fred, a psychotherapist, adopted his son Jonathan as a toddler when he was 38. Fred had a similar view. "I made a commitment to raise my child as a single person. The single parent lifestyle is too demanding and intense to involve another person and add the potential of a loss if the relationship doesn't work out."

Teresa, a recreational director who adopted when she was 46, echoes the conflict of time when dealing with the needs of a child as well as a partner: "The person that I was in a relationship with did not adjust well to my need to spend time focusing on my daughter. This caused problems and eventually was part of the reason for the end of the relationship." Like many, she reports that she did not regret the break up. She felt it was a trade-off, not a loss.

Some adoptive parents changed attitudes about relationships over time. Suzanne, a realtor who had adopted two girls, four and six, by the time she was 49 felt the girls would benefit from a male role model. She was also interested in finding a partner to share parenting. "Although I was prepared to raise my daughters as a single parent, as the years went by I felt we would benefit from my having a partner and them having a father figure. I was very close to my father when I was younger – as an adult too – and it made me sad at times that my daughters didn't have that father-daughter relationship. Several years after I adopted I began to pursue dating relationships. I quickly realized that finding a partner who would fit into our complicated lives presented some challenges. I met Charles, a therapist, and we began dating. He understood the needs of my children and was open to joining our family. The girls however, were not as quick to accept him as 'dad'.

84

We tried to make it work but ultimately Charles and I decided to part. We still remain good friends."

Laura, who had adopted her eight month old son from Ecuador when she was 34, had a good experience with an ex-boyfriend: "My old boyfriend was estranged from his own biological children but he continues to be the male role model in my son's life, even though we have not been in a relationship for the past 12 years. Our friendship has grown over the years and we are both thankful for what we have given to each other."

Jody had a similar experience: "I co-parented with a partner for the first 2½ years after the adoption, until our relationship developed problems and we separated. My daughter and my partner still have a daughter/surrogate father relationship. Currently he is supportive financially for education expenses and present for all major events in her life. Although we have both moved on, he continues to be the 'father figure' in her life."

Some who adopted children as single parents, later married. Although the complexities of the relationships between the couple as well as the children are often challenging for all those involved, many work out unique and successful parenting plans.

Roslyn, a 38 year old teacher, states: "I married my partner a year after I adopted my children. Although he was active in my children's lives, I was the primary parent. We had worked out an arrangement that seemed to be successful. I was the one who sets the limits and he offered support and spent time with the kids. We believed that honest communication and perseverance would get us through the difficult times. Now fifteen years later, my children still appreciate my husband and view him as the father figure in their lives."

Janet, a small business owner who adopted at 30, tells her story: "I loved being a single mother. I adopted two sisters from India and for a time it was the three of us, period. When I met and married a wonderful man twelve years later, followed by the birth of our daughter, the challenges began. I realized I should have better prepared my older daughters for the possibility of adding a partner and a birth child in the mix. By identifying so much as a single mother and not allowing for the possibility of marriage, the girls came to believe this is the way it would always be. When I married and had a biological daughter, they felt abandoned and betrayed. They could not readily accept the change or the addition of a new sibling. In hindsight," Janet says, "I should have insisted upon family therapy from the start of my marriage. There was so much to work through. Today, thankfully the three girls are very much bonded as sisters and though it's been a long road, we are finally at a good place as a family."

Sue, 41 when she adopted her daughter, has a unique story: "When my daughter was 8, I reconnected with my current husband at a conference in New York. We had dated in high school but I hadn't seen him in 30 years. I was in Boston and he was in San Francisco. He was divorced and had a nine year old son from that marriage. We had a long distance relationship for one year and were married the following June. We moved to D.C. to be near my stepson who was living with his mother. The first few years were hard for all of us. My stepson often resented the intrusion of myself and my daughter and my daughter was often jealous of my relationship with my husband. We somehow survived those years and both kids are off with their own lives now. The struggles have somehow made my relationship with my husband stronger. There were, however, many difficult years. We stuck with it and have come out the other end! We are now grandparents and that is another amazing benefit of the whole experience!"

Caroline, a lesbian sociology professor who at 40 adopted her two year old daughter from New Hampshire and two years later her second child, from the same agency. Nine years after the first adoption, she met and began to co-parent with her partner, Judy. "From the time my first child was 11 and my second child 7, I have been in a committed relationship, with my partner having full co-parenting responsibility. We adopted our third child together seven years later. Our family continues to work through the many challenges we have faced and I believe we have all grown as a result."

Summary

We asked the participants to identify people in their lives that provided them with support and we wanted to understand the impact of meaningful relationships in the lives of single adoptive parents and their children. The adoption community provided support in more than half of the cases. As we have seen, many parents chose their communities because of the diversity of the community which included adoptive families. Most reported that they sought and received support from other adoptive families, specifically single parent adoptive families.

Romantic relationships did not usually appear to be a source of support and in fact almost half of the participants reported these relationships had a negative effect on the lives of their children. However, 16 % of the participants who pursued romantic relationships felt these relationships were of some support to the family. Bear in mind that more than half of the participants chose not to be in a romantic relationship during the time that they were raising their children. They decided to build their social relationships around family, friends and other single parent and adoptive families.

Approximately half felt they received support from the practice of their religion and involvement in their religious community.

Friends were overwhelmingly the source of the greatest support, noted in the case of 85% of the participants, with siblings and extended family members providing support to more than 50% of the participants. Mothers (of the adoptive parent) provided support to one third of the participants and one quarter of the participants felt that their fathers were a source of support. Other single parents comprised support in 40%

of the cases. The second greatest support, in more than 70% of the families, came from other single adoptive parents. Other sources of support (40%) came from educators and therapists.

It is clear that support is critical and developing a support system is one of the most important steps in determining a successful and positive outcome for the single adoptive family.

CHAPTER SIX

Juggling Career and Parenting

When we began our decision-making groups at The Adoption Network in the 1980s we found that the first wave of single adoptive parents tended to be social workers, teachers, and healthcare workers, most notably those who worked directly with children. Over the past two decades singles from a wider variety of professions have chosen to adopt.

Still, the majority of those in our survey worked in either education or social services. Twenty-six per cent of people in our survey worked in education and 32.5% were in social services and health-related fields.

Participants in our survey were largely college educated. Only 3% said they had completed high school and had not pursued further education. Four percent had some training after high school, and 16 % had completed their bachelor's degree. The majority of participants – 57% – had masters' degrees, or other advanced degrees.

In our questionnaire we asked people what it was like to integrate their career with their role as a parent. Juggling work, whether full or part-time, and parenting, is a challenge for any parent, but for a single parent it can be more daunting. What happens when you are in a meeting or at an important job site and you get a call that your son is running a 102 degree fever or that your daughter has just been bitten by another child? In our workshops we had people fantasize these scenarios while trying to decide if they were up to the task of solo parenting.

Of the people we surveyed, 56% said that integrating their career with their role as a parent was difficult, 16% said it was neither difficult nor easy, and 28% said it was somewhat easy.

Time management

As a university professor, Sandra felt the pressures of single parenthood: "It is a constant juggling act – having to leave work to take care of doctor appointments, school visits, and kid activities; and then taking work home and doing conference calls at 9 P.M., checking voicemail and email at home at night and on the weekends." She ends by saying, "I would have loved to work part-time or not at all while raising my daughter but my finances did not allow for that option."

For teachers and others whose calendar follows the school year, it was helpful to have summers and vacations at the same time as their children. Some preferred doing freelance work or juggling several part-time jobs, while others preferred the set hours of working nine to five.

Although it was rare, some people had flexible work environments and were able to take their child to work when needed. Several people who worked at universities or colleges said they had some flexibility in their schedules.

Wanda, who works in the publishing field and was able to work several days at home when her children were young, said: "Because I'm able to work at home so much and have a great deal of flexibility in my hours, I can easily take time for appointments, attend practices and games, and go to school meetings. I can intersperse household chores throughout the day, leaving the weekends more open for family time rather than grocery shopping and laundry. However, it remains a challenge to actually work when the kids are home."

Integrating work and parenting is always a challenge for single parents. For those in demanding jobs and jobs that don't have generous vacations or flex-time options, it can be complicated. Lena, a city planner, said that her daughter had many ear infections when she was young. "I almost lost my job because I missed so much work," she said.

Most parents, whether they have a supportive workplace or not, found they had times when they worried about their children while at work. For many, it wasn't easy to check in during the day. This was more difficult before the 1990s when cell phones and text messaging were not in common use. Michael, a painter and contractor who adopted his first child in 1975, said it was difficult to get to a phone during the day and he worried about his children while at work.

Parents who were on the "fast track" at work before adopting often had to adjust their priorities. Those who had been in demanding jobs frequently had to re-evaluate how they spent their time and energy after adopting. Susan, a television producer, found it difficult to work in television full-time and be a single mom. "I had to work days that were too long – often 12 hours plus commute. I spent a fortune on childcare and I was constantly juggling childcare providers. Babysitters would pick my daughter up at daycare and often have to feed her and put her to bed. There were days when I would come home exhausted having spent no quality time with my child. I began to realize the stress was too great for both of us. I didn't become a mother to spend so little time with my child. It wasn't fair to either of us. I decided to take a less demanding position, with regular hours. My priority was my daughter."

Jobs that required long hours, long commutes, or travel are difficult for single parents and their children.

For all adopted children loss is an issue – they have already lost their first parents and usually they have been separated from other caregivers as well. Extended absences of a parent can be difficult for them. Even when there is a family member or regular caregiver, especially in the first few years while the child is adjusting to their new parent and environment, these absences can be difficult for both child and parent. Parents also feel the loss. They have waited a long time for the opportunity to parent and want to be available to their children.

If parents bring their children along when they travel for work, new issues can arise. Sandra was often asked to attend conferences in other states. She spoke about the difficulties of combining a demanding job with her role as a parent: "I took my daughter on several trips for work that lasted two or three days. Each time I had to locate a babysitter in different cities and negotiate airports. It was a challenge that I learned to rise to. But it was exhausting and could not continue when my daughter got older."

Single parents found it especially difficult to find time for themselves while attempting to integrate parenting and careers. As a working single parent, many felt pressed for time.

While Sarah had holidays and summers off to be with her daughter, she often found it difficult to integrate her career with her role as a parent: "I brought work home nightly," she said. "I couldn't start my 'homework' until my daughter was asleep and the household chores were completed. It was hard to get enough sleep!"

Jill explains: "Being a single mother, working full time, and being solely responsible for the mortgage, healthcare costs, daily living expenses, etc…was at times exhausting. It was important to have a solid routine, and I was extremely fortunate to have my aunt as a caregiver for Kim."

In addition to finding little time for themselves, single adoptive parents are often trapped in the *sandwich generation* – trying to attend to the needs of aging parents while raising young children. Karen, 42 when she adopted her four year old daughter, struggled to regularly visit her parents in an assisted living facility while raising her daughter who had special needs. "I felt like a yo-yo at times – I had to advocate for my parents on the one hand and my child on the other."

A single adoptive parent doesn't have a partner to take over when needed. Therefore, along with a support network of friends and family, good childcare is crucial. Many singles devised ingenious ways to find such help. Kelly, a special needs teacher who adopted at 38, hired a young college student who, in exchange for room and board, was available to help with childcare.

Wanda, an educational publisher, worked at home three days a week and made a two hour-long commute on the other two days. The fact that she had three weeks' vacation and ten paid holidays helped to make up for the strain of the commute. She thought of moving closer to work. However, her mother was always available to care for her children when Wanda had to travel for work. The children grew close to their grandmother who provided the support Wanda needed to balance work and single parenting.

Expect the unexpected

Some single parents faced their own health issues. For those with a health problem that compromised their energy or ability to function, the demands of parenting were often difficult, particularly if they lacked a good support system. Paula, a lawyer who adopted at 32 was diagnosed with diabetes two years later. She wrote that it was especially difficult to integrate career and raising a child while trying to keep her diabetes under control. She had to take insulin injections three times a day and watch her diet carefully.

As all parents know, things don't always go as expected. One adopts and finds out her child has special needs, requiring extra care and intervention. One becomes disabled or ill and is unable to work or take care of her child. Even if nothing out of the ordinary occurs, becoming a parent for the first time can be overwhelming. You may have dreamed and planned for the moment when you would meet your child, and suddenly find you feel unexpectedly sad or even panicked. For singles, a feeling of isolation and the realization that they are really on their own may suddenly hit them.

Single people found many sources of support that made a significant difference in their adjustment to parenting and in dealing with unexpected events. Good childcare and a solid support network were most frequently cited as helping coordinate parenting and employment. Having supportive co-workers, a flexible schedule, and proximity to work so commute time was minimized, were also cited as helpful factors when raising a child on your own.

Marnie, a special education advocate, adopted her first child at 28. By the time she was 34, she was the mother of four adopted children. She feels the best advice is to expect the unexpected. "It is always necessary to look ahead and to try to pre-plan for the unexpected. A single mom wears many hats… and flexibility and maintaining a sense of humor are necessary survival skills!!"

Many singles emphasized that having good health insurance, disability insurance, and working for a company that is family-friendly and allows flexible time off is a big help. An understanding boss is always helpful. Although rare, the option of bringing a child to work if necessary is a significant benefit.

Perhaps one of the most important ways for parents to integrate their professional lives and parenting was to have a solid support network. While having caring family members nearby was a huge help, many single parents had family that wasn't available or lived far away. The majority of single parents found it easiest to find other single parents who were interested in creating a support network.

Priorities

Although most single parents remained at the same job after they adopted their child(ren), their relationship to work often changed. For many singles, their careers had been the focal point of their lives. After adopting this often changed. Linda turned down several promotions at the social service agency she worked for because she wanted to have time for her sons: "I was always a committed worker who went the extra mile," she said. "After adopting my sons, I had to leave on time and could not put in extra hours. That was very difficult for me, yet I also felt I needed more time with my sons. There was a constant conflict between my role as a mother and my job responsibilities." Several singles echoed Linda's sentiment and also said they turned down promotions in order to have a more flexible schedule and more time with their kids.

Several parents noted some advantages of a single parent household for their children and themselves. For example, children often needed to pitch in and help out and this fostered a sense of responsibility and independence in them. Many parents were open with their children about their struggle to juggle work life with parenting, and they felt it helped their children to have a more realistic sense about life and to develop coping mechanisms.

Michael, who adopted several children, said: "My household was very democratic. We had family meetings and assigned each person responsibilities. Everyone got a share in decision-making unless it was a decision only the parent (myself) could make. We decided where we would go on trips together and also who would mow the lawn."

Economic Resources

The majority of people who responded to our questionnaire had what would be considered middle class incomes while raising their children. Ninety-nine percent said that their job was the main source of their income.

Of those we contacted, 83 % were employed full-time while raising their children, and 16% were employed part- time and 1% were not working. Those who were unemployed had other means of support such as an inheritance, government subsidies or family help.

Single people who adopt tend to be resourceful and self-sufficient, and often have a make-do attitude. Still, it is amazing to learn just how resourceful some of them were while raising their children. The majority, 56%, made between $55,000 and $100,000, while raising their child(ren). 16% per cent made between $20,000 and $55,000 and 28% made less than $20,000. It should be noted that the period of time we are referring to was from the late '70s to the early '90s.

Despite financial stressors and the need to budget carefully, many singles said they had achieved a degree of financial stability before they decided to adopt and this proved helpful. Several singles we spoke with said the stability of their job and financial situation gave them the confidence to adopt. Those with a stable profession and adequate financial resources reported that economic security was crucial in raising their children. Many single parents felt that owning their own home or condo was something that provided security for themselves and their child(ren).

Some parents felt having only one income with which to raise their child(ren), while challenging, helped them become resourceful and inventive. Linda said: "I had no problem asking for financial aid for sports, camp, and school activities.

Linda explained, "Fortunately, we lived in a town that offered lots of recreational and sports activities, many of which were free, and also offered scholarships to low income families. We bought a lot of sports equipment second-hand and some of it was donated."

When a degree of financial stability was achieved, single adoptive parents often put money into college savings. Maria, an educational specialist who adopted at 39, faithfully put money into her daughter's education fund so that she could "earn an education as debt-free as possible."

Finances often determine the decision to adopt again. Sarah said: "Economic resources influenced my need to work full-time and also determined where we lived. I would have adopted more children if I had the financial backing to do so." Sarah was not alone in this sentiment. Several people said they would have adopted again if the financial resources had been greater.

In our questionnaire we asked to what degree financial resources were a source of stress or worry while parenting. Twenty-eight percent said little or not at all, 48% said somewhat, and 24% said very much.

Linda wrote that finances played a huge part in raising her children: "We can't do a lot of things that other families with two incomes do, like go to Disney World and buy the latest and greatest of everything." She went on to say that while her children are not deprived, "I make them very aware of the cost of everything and have them save to buy big ticket luxury items."

Most single adoptive parents said they had to prioritize their spending. Linda added that after adopting Richie and Jessie she became more frugal. "I rarely used babysitters for anything other than going to work-related meetings at night. Although there were some tough times, we managed to get through them."

Knowing there were family members or friends to rely on was a great comfort to single parents who were lucky enough to have that support. Although Grace's mother and sisters lived far away, having their emotional and financial support was invaluable. As she said, "having family who could have rescued me, had I needed it, allowed me not to face parenthood balanced on the shaky pedestal of financial fear."

Claire said: "Although adoption as a single parent has brought extraordinary joy and richness to living, this experience asks for a multitude of emotional and financial resources. It's helpful to have enough financial resources to be able to give yourself a break when needed – dinner out, vacations, babysitters, therapists."

Jill, mother of Kim talks about finances as the "most difficult part of being a single parent." She advises, "Save money!! Some married couples have only one income too, but if one spouse is not working there is no need for daycare. For singles, we are hit with a double-whammy – just one income and daycare. If you have a nest egg, you have emergency funds to fall back on. Also, develop a small network of people you can count on. Find someone so that, when you are deathly ill with the flu and need someone to take your child for the day, they will be there. It's also important to have someone to share the proud moments of your little sweetheart's, first steps, graduation, soccer goal, that *A* in chemistry. You don't need scores of people or a huge family, just two or three really caring and supportive relatives and/or friends are plenty."

Even when finances were adequate, single adoptive parents noted that they were careful with their economic resources. Although the financial burden of raising a child as a single parent can be considerable most who choose to adopt find a way to manage their budgets and make things work. Single adoptive parents have demonstrated ingenuity and resourcefulness when making ends meet.

CHAPTER SEVEN

Special Needs of Single Adoptive Families

There is no question that parenting is challenging. Parenting as a single person and parenting through adoption can bring added layers of complexity. While the great majority of singles in our survey felt positive with their decision to adopt on their own, many felt, at times, overwhelmed with the added burden of being the primary provider, decision-maker, disciplinarian and nurturer.

Facing the challenges

Marylyn, a small business owner and mother of two girls, spoke about the challenges of single parenting. "Feeling like there is no one there when you are tired or sick with no safe place to fall. You have no one with whom to split duties. Only yourself to drop off and pick up the kids, pay the bills, get the oil changed, mow the grass (or make enough money to pay someone else), cook or make or buy breakfast, lunch, and dinner, take them to the doctors and dentists, oversee the homework, manage the parental controls (on internet, instant messaging, television), soothe the crying child whose feelings have been hurt, run the child (or your parent) to the emergency room while dragging the other child(ren) along, master the digital camera or video camera or decide to forgo it because you would rather stay in the moment, drive the car while you mediate the fight in the back seat, change all of the disposable diapers, sell the house and buy the new one, go to all the parent-teacher nights and assemble the toys at midnight on Christmas Eve, be the tooth fairy, Santa Claus, Easter Bunny, etc., (and) try to find ways to make sure that your family and friends understand that your role has changed. You will no longer be the *go-to* person."

Claire describes her experience as a single parent: "You are on 24/7 – from getting them off to school in the morning to helping with homework and putting them to bed at night."

Even for those married or with a helpful partner, there are times when exhaustion seems to go hand-in-hand with parenting. As Claire said, "One of the hardest parts of parenting is finding those fifteen minutes of undisturbed time - so I can regain the perspective to be the parent I always wanted to be. I wanted to be a mom and knew I could be a better mother if I made some time for myself."

It isn't just a second income that would make a difference for many single parents, it is the desire to have time for oneself, even a few minutes to be able to breathe deeply and feel more refreshed.

A new mom at the age of 42, Sandra talks about how she "readied herself" for the upcoming challenges she knew she would face with the decision to adopt. "As

106

an older parent-to-be, I knew that my mom wouldn't be able to help much because of her age. I would need to ensure that I had a 'family of choice' - friends to be there for me in case of need."

Prior to the arrival of her six year old daughter Lissette, Sandra connected to other single parents at her church. It was this group of people that welcomed her daughter home. "Some of the church families got together and had a "Welcome Home" party for Lissette and me. I was so touched. They continue to provide ongoing support and a sense of family. Holidays, birthdays, and other special occasions were shared with this new found family 'of choice'. We visited my family in California twice a year and they visited us during the summer. It's amazing how everything just fell into place."

Grace advises that you "improve your physical fitness before adoption, identify resources such as childcare and a pediatrician (if it's an international adoption - someone experienced with internationally adopted children) ahead of time, get rested, and go on a real vacation. Join an adoption group, read and become knowledgeable about adoption and child development issues."

Time and money were issues that came up again and again. Most single adoptive parents have full time jobs. Therefore, finding good childcare is critical to support their busy lifestyle. Those that reported close support networks seemed to cope with the challenges of single parenting better.

"Parenting will take over your life," Michael said. "Make sure that that's in line with your values and the way you want to spend your time. On the other hand, parenting won't necessarily turn you into a hermit - you can keep doing a lot of what you valued doing before, but modified to incorporate kids(s). If that sounds good to you, go for it! Be as sure as you can that this life-long commitment is what you want and what is best for your adopted child."

Therapeutic issues

Post-Adoption Depression Syndrome, (PADS) is a term coined by June Bond, an adoption advocate. While not going through the hormonal ups and downs following pregnancy, adoptive parents do go through a shift in their identity and can feel overwhelmed by the demands of a new child. Jennifer, at 32, had adopted a newborn. She marveled, "When I brought my daughter home I suddenly realized how alone I was. I was overwhelmed and wondered if I had done the right thing."

It is important not to bottle up these feelings and to find safe places, such as adoption support groups where you can share your feelings and hear that others are going through similar challenges.

The cost of therapy, special schools, tutoring or other services can be expensive. Matthew was adopted by Grace at birth. After several months, Grace, a doctor, noticed that Matthew was having difficulty making sounds and responding to noises. At his first medical examination, the doctor raised concerns about his hearing. Grace was surprised as she had known the birthmother, Tammy, and knew she had had excellent prenatal care. After a thorough evaluation, however, Matthew was diagnosed with a moderate hearing impairment. At first Grace was distraught. However, she was determined to find the best possible services to help her son. "Because I have a child with special needs," she said "I have paid more for childcare, specialized camps, and tutors."

Some children who are adopted domestically may come with adoption subsidies that cover some expenses; others may be eligible for programs such as Early Intervention, Title IV-E and even Medicaid. However, many children do not come with subsidies and are not eligible for any kind of financial assistance. Parents need to depend on support and creative solutions to address these needs.

While single parenting itself can be challenging, it can be especially difficult when children have special needs. Some of the parents who responded to our survey noted that their children had a diagnosis before the adoption, allowing parents to have some idea of what to expect. The majority were diagnosed once the child was home. Although the children's conditions were often mild or moderate, some of the issues were more severe.

Claire, who adopted two year old Nadia from Romania, had not anticipated the difficulty she would experience adjusting to her new environment. The limited information Claire received, suggested Nadia had spent her first two years in an institution. She seemed to have difficulty trusting and forming a connection with Claire and her new sister, Eva. In fact, when Claire tried to hold Nadia, she began crying and pushed her away avoiding eye contact. Claire said, "Mealtimes were particularly difficult. Nadia often refused to eat most foods, yet later she would find food hidden in her room. Social situations and transitions were fraught with tension. She frequently had tantrums when other children tried to use her toys and often lashed out at them. To soothe herself she would sit in a corner and rock. Other kids and even some parents were afraid of hers behavior. It broke my heart to see this and furthered a sense of isolation." On the advice of a therapist specializing in adoption, Claire requested a full evaluation by her local public school. Nadia was placed in an Early Intervention Program and began to receive speech, occupational and play therapy. Claire met with a group of other parents whose children were also experiencing attachment issues. She felt validated and supported and regained her sense of hope. Claire adds, "Over the years I have come to accept my daughter's challenges and in fact being her mom has helped me to grow as a person. I am more understanding and patient with myself and my children. I have adjusted my expectations and it's helped to connect with parents of children with similar challenges."

Linda's two sons were both diagnosed with ADHD (attention deficit hyperactivity disorder) and other learning disabilities. "Both my boys are energetic and love sports. I made sure they got the services they needed in school and had opportunities to develop their skills in sports and creative arts. The issue of the boys attending college was no longer my dream. Providing my children with opportunities to develop positive self-esteem became the goal."

As adoptive parents we are glad to finally have achieved our dream of becoming a parent. We may forget, that in the midst of our joy our child may be mourning the loss of people and places they have left behind. Even if the child is leaving a neglectful or abusive setting, there can still be a profound sense of sadness at the loss of what was familiar. One mother who adopted a four year-old girl spoke of her daughter's "innate sadness at the change in her surroundings and culture." Her daughter would often cry herself to sleep at night. She was reluctant to discuss her feelings surrounding her adoption, either with her mother or in therapy.

It is helpful for parents to begin speaking about adoption with their children when they are young so that hopefully, the child will feel comfortable voicing questions and concerns as they arise. While not forcing the subject of adoption it is important to provide opportunities for open discussion so that it can normalize adoption. Reading adoption related children's books as well as books which discuss talking with your child about adoption, and interacting with other adoptive families can be helpful (See appendix for a list of some children's books).

There are times when it is difficult to determine if the behaviors of adopted children are a specific result of being adopted. Adoptive parents may wonder if their children are experiencing problematic behaviors as a result of the adoption process, or if he is simply going through "normal" developmental stages, or as a result of a combination of both factors.

For some parents, there is a tendency to attribute an overabundance of behaviors to the child's adoption. While not wanting to overlook behaviors that are, in fact, due to adoption, it is important to try to distinguish these from normal issues of development. Discerning the difference between the two can be a challenge for the adoptive parent as well as the professionals. This is one reason many adoptive parents connect themselves with a community of other adoptive parents and professionals, who are familiar with families dealing with adoption. Adoptive parents must learn to be advocates, educating those who interact with their children.

Most parents of teens will agree that these can be challenging years. When children begin to assert more independence, the ensuing struggles between parent and child can be intense. One mother commented, "It's hard not to take things personally." While infancy can bring sleepless nights, the teen years can often bring emotional exhaustion. As children venture out into the world, making their own choices, learning to drive and to date,

112

single parents are often alone navigating through this uncertain time.

Linda wrote: "I find the challenges and aloneness I feel dealing with adolescent behavior to be more draining than during toddler days when the challenges were more physical. By this time of life, the support available to help with a 'cute' toddler has gone away. There are far less friends willing to help with adolescent issues."

Sarah agrees: "Definitely, adolescence was the most challenging time. It was a period in our relationship where I questioned single parenthood. My daughter and I made it through this period somehow and came out of it unscathed. But there were many occasions I wished I had a partner in my life that could have backed up some of my unpopular decisions."

Sarah added that what was difficult about her daughter's adolescence was "learning to control my anger when my daughter would push me to the limit… to hold in angry words that I would later regret saying."

Many parents, whether through birth or adoption, whether single or with a partner, have felt bouts of guilt. Guilt that they couldn't always be there for their children, guilt over things they may have said or done in a moment of exhaustion or anger. Having our children witness our struggles may at times prove to be beneficial. Seeing how we deal with our own limitations may help them to understand how to deal with their own struggles.

Meeting with a therapist can be helpful. It is just as natural for children to have issues related to their adoption – issues that change over time – as it is for parents to have their own concerns. A therapist's knowledge in adoption issues can be a valuable support during difficult times. There are also many excellent books on adoption, for both parents and children, which can be useful in navigating parenting as a single adoptive parent. (See appendix).

Finding the right therapist or school setting is important. Linda, a social worker well-versed in attachment issues notes, "Children who are adopted when they are older may come with a lot of trauma. The mental health field in general is limited in their ability to address the issues adoptive parents face. It is advisable to find a therapist who is knowledgeable about adoption issues."

Michael, who adopted his children when they were school-age, openly shares his personal experience. "Adoptive families have different problems. Things just don't always go smoothly without extra effort. Having unrealistic expectations of your child's accomplishments may cause unnecessary friction between you and your child and threaten his or her self-esteem."

Race, culture, and integrating past and present

"When I first adopted Graciela from El Salvador," said Sarah, "I felt threatened by the fear of her biological parents wanting her back. In hindsight, it

114

is the one thing (my daughter's biological parents), regrettably, that I cannot give to my child. The possibility of knowing them would be a great gift and the key to unlocking much of her history that will likely be lost forever." Adopted children come with history, even newborns. Having that history is a birthright and becomes important in the lives of many adoptees. Being conscious of and sensitive to what adoption means to your child is essential. Adoptive parents are sometimes threatened at the thought of a reunion between their adopted child and the birthparent. Yet, studies show the connection with the birthparent often helps strengthen the relationship between the adoptee and their adoptive parents. Further, learning more about the birth family can help to integrate past and present and provide some of the missing pieces of their identity. In addition, it can provide a wealth of family history and medical information. In some cases, both the adoptive family and the birth family form a bond.

Claire, who adopted two year old Nadia from Romania, feels that, "It is important to safeguard any information you have concerning your child's family of origin and birth culture. I wish I had kept a journal and made more effort to keep and maintain cultural ties. It becomes more important with time."

An elementary school teacher who adopted her two daughters at the ages of six and four from Haiti when she was 52 expressed her wish that she had known more about attachment issues: "I would have worked harder at creating a deeper bond. I thought it would naturally occur, but there were some serious walls up. I didn't realize it at the time. I would have worked harder to locate Haitian families as my children never had Haitian role models."

The theme of staying connected with a child's birth culture was common among survey participants. Whether your child was adopted domestically or from another country, it can be advantageous to gather information and support the adoptee in the exploration of their background. Timing however is important. Parents should be sensitive to their child's feelings and not "push" a reunion or investigation of their past until the adoptee feels ready.

Adopted at age seven from Honduras, Rosa and her mother went back to visit her orphanage. Rosa describes the experience as important. "My mom really wanted to make the trip. I didn't think I would find any of my relatives but just being there brought back memories. I remembered smells and places I visited. I even reconnected with a nun who always made me feel special. Although I was reluctant to go, I have to admit it was a great experience. The only thing that bothered me was that my Spanish was poor. I'm glad I had the opportunity to go, but thankful to return home with my mom."

Nelson was adopted as an infant during the civil war in El Salvador. During a difficult period in Nelson's adolescence, his mother felt that finding out more information about his birth family might help him to have a better sense of where he had come from and who he was. "I was hoping this connection might be the 'missing piece' of the puzzle he seemed to be seeking. Unfortunately, in hindsight, I think I was premature in my actions. To my surprise, although his parents were both deceased, I was able to make contact with several of his siblings who happened to have migrated to a city not far from where we were living. I told my son I had made contact and wanted him to meet his brothers and sisters. Although the meeting went well and they were overjoyed to see him, he was very angry with me for having pushed him into this reunion. For several years he had no contact with them and I was the only one who stayed in touch. In time however, he was able to forgive me. I was filled with emotion when years later he told me he was grateful that I had reached out to his family and he began to develop a relationship with them."

While the singles we contacted were mainly Caucasian, many of them adopted African American, biracial, Latino or Asian children. For some, adopting a child of a different race or ethnicity was the first time they came face to face with racism. Roz, a Caucasian mother of a Hispanic child, acknowledged this fact: "It came as a shock to realize how racist our culture is and how this affects our children's experience in the world. People are amazingly ignorant and often make hurtful, stupid comments. It singles out our children and points a finger at their difference. For my daughter it served as a steady reminder that she didn't belong and it wore away at her already fragile sense of self."

Grace, having adopted a biracial infant added. "As a white mother, raising a child of color in this culture I have come face to face with the challenges. My sense is that my child is exhausted by the constant questions and his need to explain our family. I am angered by this culture and the gross inequality for anybody who isn't part of the white dominant culture. White privilege is alive and well, and often excludes many."

Others have had very different experiences. Karen who moved from a predominately white suburb in Massachusetts to Memphis, Tennessee states, "We never experienced any overt racism. I am white and my two daughters are African American. We have always had friends of all races and I made sure our social network was diverse so that it helped offset the fact that they were often the only children of color in their elementary school classes. Race has not been a major issue in our lives. Our sense of community and close family ties seem to trump the ignorance of society and prejudice that continues to exist."

Some adoptive parents find that racist views exist within their own families. At times, parents, siblings and extended family are reluctant to accept a child of another race into the family. In our experience, however, most family members do "come around" and are ultimately supportive. Some however may be less than welcoming to a child and less than supportive to the new parent. Such reactions can be difficult. As a mother of a Latino child said, "My mother was very negative about the idea of my adopting a child at all, and particularly a child from a different ethnicity. Although she eventually did form a relationship with my son, she continued to make racially insensitive remarks, and I had to risk losing our relationship when I told her I couldn't tolerate this. It was very hard for me since my son adored his grandmother."

Just as negative stereotypes can be hurtful to self-esteem, so called 'positive' or apparently benign stereotypes can also affect a child's sense of self. For example, African Americans are good at sports or Asians are good in math and science are typical stereotypes which can place undue pressure on a child.

One mother of an adolescent teen stated: "Because my son was African American and tall for his age, people just assumed he would be a star basketball player. His gym teacher really pushed him to go out for the team telling him "With your height, you could be the next Michael Jordan". Jason was feeling a lot of pressure and one day came home in tears saying he hated basketball. In fact Jason was somewhat of a computer nerd and never seemed particularly interested in sports. I realized the mistake I had made in allowing the coach to put pressure on my son. Soon after he quit basketball and began spending his time with computer games. As parents who have adopted trans-racially, we need to be alert to any signs of racism and/or stereotyping, and be ready to intervene or advocate for our children when needed."

Jill adopted Kim as an infant from China. "Even as a young child she was loud and boisterous. Although Jill appreciated her daughter's effervescent spirit, it was often disruptive to others. One day in church when Kim was particularly restless, a woman turned to her and said, 'I thought little Chinese girls were supposed to be well-behaved.' I was so stunned," Jill said, "I didn't know what to say. I always knew stereotyping was harmful, and this brought it to a personal level. The expectation that my daughter should be demure and soft spoken, was ludicrous and limiting to her self-image."

Conclusions

We conclude with the advice we have heard from some single adoptive parents.

"If this is what you really want – go for it! Everything will fall into place. Make sure you have good support – you will have those bad days sneak up. Prepare for a major change in life!"

Even with all the challenges inherent in single parent adoption, 95% of the parents interviewed stated they were greatly satisfied with their decision to adopt. As one mom put it, "So if you are considering adoption as a single parent, start the process now – you can always slow it down, or decide against it after you get the information – but you can't speed it up. Be fully informed of services, (social and health), for children and families. Talk with a variety of people with adopted children to hear experiences and information regarding adoption issues, and participate in organizations and groups that nurture family strengths. Be prepared to make adoption your main focus in life. It is not an easy road, but it is filled with love, fun, and new friends."

CHAPTER EIGHT

The Joys

Despite the many challenges of single adoptive parenthood, the majority of parents felt happy with their lives and said that the joys of parenting outweighed the difficult aspects. On a scale of 1 to 10 (1 being the least and 10 being the most), when asked how happy they were with their lives, 61% reported overall satisfaction between 9 and 10, 31% reported being between 7 and 8, and 8% reported being between 4 and 6. When asked, "How satisfied are you with your decision to adopt as a single parent?" 84% rated themselves between 9 and 10, 12% rated themselves between 7 and 8, and 4% rated themselves between 4 and 6.

Many parents spoke in superlatives when describing the joys of parenting. As Jill said: "Adopting my daughter has been the most rewarding experience of my life. We have an incredibly strong bond and are very close."

Sandra wrote of the joy of parenthood: "The love that my child and I shared from day one has been the greatest happiness I could have hoped for in life. Each memory of her childhood brings a smile to my face. We both have been blessed by the experience of single parent adoption and reap the benefits even now as she matures into a beautiful young woman."

Grace wrote: "being the mother of my son is truly the most fulfilling experience of my life. The pleasure that motherhood has brought me has been monumental. I am at peace with my life."

Along with creating a family of their own, singles most frequently cited the deep emotional connections they felt with their children as one of the most gratifying aspects of parenting. Singles often said they didn't mind giving up what one woman termed "the self-centeredness of single life," in order to raise children. The happiness that single adoptive parents felt at sharing in their children's lives, seeing them develop and mature into adulthood was extremely rewarding. This did not mean things always went smoothly. Yet, whether people had children with greater or fewer needs, they still spoke of their deep emotional connections with their children as an important part of parenthood.

As Michael, the father of five, said: "I love being a dad and have never regretted my decision to adopt. Having children makes life worthwhile. Each and every child is unique and the emotional bond is so special!" Referring to the close relationship shared with his children, he added: "They're all adults and still end phone calls with 'I love you.'"

Celebrating the journey

Many singles spoke of the happiness they felt in nurturing a child emotionally as well as physically. Watching their children grow and develop; sharing the child's milestones and triumphs, whether this was losing a first tooth or skating across an ice rink by themselves, starting the first day at school clutching their lunchbox or graduating from college – these were some of the rewarding memories parents recalled.

As we have seen, many who adopted on their own are in the teaching or helping professions, and to some extent all parents are teachers and counselors when it comes to raising their children. Men and women who adopted on their own spoke of valuing the opportunities they had as parents to model and teach important life values. Linda said: "I enjoyed teaching the boys new things and talking to them about the values I feel are important. Together we helped out at our church's meals program for the homeless. This was something important we shared. Today the boys are both employed. They are productive and helping to make the world a better place. Richie works as a sexton in a church and Jessie works for a food bank. They both take a lot of pride in their work."

Claire states, "Nadia was a challenging child. I have tried to instill the value of hard work and perseverance. As a teen, things didn't come easy to her and she lost many jobs because of her explosive behavior. Finally, she was taken under the wing of the cook in the cafeteria where she was working. She went to culinary school and has held the same job for many years. I am really proud of her."

Single adoptive parents often spoke about the joy of watching their children move through different stages of development. Jill, whose daughter is now a budding actress in New York, wrote that the most positive thing about raising her daughter on her own was: "The simple joy of loving an amazing child and lending myself to her growth and development."

Adolescence, with its issues around identity, can be a tumultuous time for adoptive parents. We have seen in the previous chapter, how difficult and trying this time can be, often pushing parents to their limits. However, many single adoptive parents also spoke about the exhilaration of seeing their children become adults and begin to live their own lives. Grace said: "It is an incredible gift to watch my son mature! I love being his mom."

Sarah said: "I've loved being a parent. It was great when Graciela was little – the zoo trips, reading books, giving baths – everything. But I think it's great that she is now an adult. At this point, we're best of friends, although sometimes she still needs me to be 'mom.'"

Michael said there were many gratifying times with his five children – among the highlights were his daughter's wedding and his son running in the Special Olympics.

Eileen is now 80 and has raised two children as well as several grandchildren. She said that the most positive thing about her decision to adopt on her own was "watching my children, both of whom came from difficult and impoverished situations, grow into responsible adults, and celebrating their achievements."

Many felt joy at seeing their children blossom into adults. One mother of a daughter adopted from China spoke about "watching her daughter grow into a kind-hearted teen," and another mom spoke about the positive experience of "seeing my son grow into an independent young man."

Janis, the mother of two daughters from Colombia, said: "being a parent has given me the experience of being intimate with children. I do not own them, but for a while, was able to guide them, enjoy their company, influence them and now see them grow into wonderful young women. It's very satisfying and fulfilling."

Barbara said: "It has been the single best thing I have ever done with my life. For people who want children, there is nothing that can replace the love of a child and the thrill that comes from watching your child grow."

A purposeful life

Several singles spoke about the joys of this unconditional love. Ruth, mother of one daughter, cited the most positive experience of single adoptive parenthood as, "Knowing unconditional love, both as a giver and a receiver." She also delighted in "seeing pure joy through my daughter – just simple, uncomplicated happiness."

It should come as no surprise that people who adopt on their own value the role of being a parent. Allison wrote: "Being a mom has exceeded all of my expectations. My life feels complete now. My daughter has enriched my life and given it purpose."

Linda said that apart from the joy of loving her children and feeling the love reciprocated, one of the best things about adopting on her own was knowing "my purpose in life."

Kris, now 62, also felt that adopting her child gave her life purpose: "My life would have been so empty without parenting my daughter and having her in my life."

One mom said that when she adopted she felt as if she was "joining the ranks of 'parents' and experiencing those universal roles of parenting that I used to look in on from the outside."

Maturing as we parent

Many singles spoke about the ways they themselves had grown and changed through the experience of parenting their child(ren). The mother of two daughters from El Salvador, said, "Single parenting has challenged me to grow as an individual in ways a career cannot do."

Jill said: "Parenting has forced me to become a better person. My value system has changed, and I am less of a perfectionist than I used to be. My life is better balanced – it is impossible to be a single parent and a workaholic."

Sandra spoke of discovering her own courage and strength as well as her ability to overcome obstacles through parenting her child. "My daughter was my focus in life and I developed greater compassion for others through the experience of parenting. Being a parent has put a clear perspective on what is important in my life. My daughter, with whom I am very close, has unwittingly taught me more about myself than almost anyone else."

Many single parents also noted that the experience of single parenthood was empowering and showed them what was possible in their lives. Grace, now nearly 60 said: "It is wonderful to know that a dream to be a parent can be fulfilled, even if you don't have a spouse to share this experience." Another mom, who had a daughter with special needs, spoke of adopting as being an empowering experience and added, "having a child to raise is an honor and a privilege."

Solo Parenting – the positive side

In the previous chapter we saw many of the challenges of single parenting. But, while there were times when single adoptive parents may have longed for a shoulder to lean on, or another set of hands to chip in, many spoke about the positive aspects of parenting on their own. A teacher, who had had numerous romantic relationships prior to adopting her daughter, said of solo parenting: "I didn't have the hassle of a recalcitrant and self-absorbed partner. One reason I adopted as a single is that the man I lived with for many years could not abide the fact that a child would command a significant amount of my attention." She appreciated being able to make the decisions that were essential for her and her daughter's lives.

A mother of three daughters, said: "My daughters and I have a great life together in our all-girl house! Now that they are all school-aged we are on the run constantly with sports and other activities, but if we want to grab fast food for dinner it's okay! If we want to sleep really, really late one Sunday morning it's okay! If we want to trek through the mall for hours just window-shopping, we can do that too. In many ways, being a good single parent carries less pressure than having to cope with also being a good spouse. You learn to be strong and independent – my daughters and I went on a family camping trip recently, pitched our own tent, cooked our own food, and had our own fun!"

Claire put it very succinctly: "The downside of adopting on your own is, 'I am responsible for everything' and the upside is, 'I am responsible for everything' – there is no one second guessing me."

Ann felt positive about having no co-parent to fight/negotiate with over raising her children. She said: "Not having to run every decision by another or to have to compromise on how I think things should go has its pros and cons; for me, more pros."

130

Another mother of two daughters said: "With all the trials and tribulations while raising the girls, I would never have passed up the experience. As I've always been a single parent, I can't really imagine raising children any other way. Having the opportunity to parent on my own has been a blessing."

New communities

Singles spoke often about how adoption had broadened their community of friends. While it's true that some friendships might have ended after becoming a parent, many people spoke about forming connections with those supportive of their new family. Jill put it this way: "Adoption has brought me many wonderful new friendships and opportunities to expand my life. While some people complain that parenting tends to limit one's opportunities, I feel it has expanded mine."

Often other single adoptive parents play a key role in one's support community. As one mom said, "Some amazing people have chosen to become single adoptive parents."

Sometimes relationships with friends or family changed for the better after adopting. Relationships with friends change and often take on new dimensions. Jill's aunt and uncle became very involved in raising Kim. Many members of Sandra's church became extended family for Sandra and Lizette. Sarah developed strong ties with other single adoptive parents, and one became Godmother to Graciela.

Michael said he felt more connected with his family after adopting his children. "Carrying out family traditions and building on them was very rewarding. My family (parents, siblings, nephews, nieces and their families) all welcomed my children."

Grace found that she needed people more after she adopted, and this proved to have some unexpectedly positive consequences. She explained: "Becoming 'needy' actually helped me to bond in deep relationships with some friends. I was very real and authentic. I wasn't pretending to have it all together. I couldn't. I needed their help. To this day – 22 years later – my child is loved deeply by friends who helped care for her since the very beginning."

Those who adopted from another country noted the positive aspects of sharing their child's culture with a community of parents whose children shared the same birth country. Many parents and their children had reunions with the families who had traveled together on their adoption trips, and they celebrated festivals and cultural events together. Sometimes they chose to visit their child's birth country together. In either case, these cultural events broadened their perspective and became something they could share with their child(ren).

For those whose children had grown and had children of their own, many talked about the joy of being a grandparent. As Sandra, now 69 said, "Being a grandmother is tremendously fulfilling, as is watching my daughter as a giving, thoughtful and loving mother.

In summary

Single adoptive parents often spoke in superlatives when describing the joys of parenthood. Phrases like "it's the best thing I have ever done," and "I couldn't imagine my life without my child(ren)" rang true for many of the single parents who wrote about their experiences. By becoming a parent, many singles felt they had found their purpose in life. They had the empowering – and cherished – opportunity of helping their children grow and develop; while they personally grew as a result of all they learned through the process of parenting and from the unconditional love they were able to experience.

CHAPTER NINE

Our Children Speak Out

The last chapter of this book has been devoted to the adult children of single adoptive parents. These adult adoptees answered a brief survey that asked them their age and year of adoption, and four questions regarding the pros and cons of adoption and adoption by a single parent. The following are their responses.

The individuals were adopted between the ages of eleven days old to eleven years. They represent five countries and three states within the US. We are most thankful to those individuals who were willing to openly tell their stories, albeit perhaps painful at times. Identifying information has been changed to respect the confidentiality of the participants.

Juana

Juana, a 36 year-old female, was born in South America and adopted at the age of seven.

Were there positive aspects of being adopted?

Yes, definitely there were positive aspects of being adopted. My family took me out of the poverty life that I was brought into. They took me out of the disasters around me and that would lead my way in the future. They took out the anger that I had inside of me.

They taught me a different way of life. They taught me love, appreciation, respect, and to be thoughtful.

Were there positive aspects of being adopted by a single person?

To be honest, you can't really say yes because if you only had one way of living then that's what you've been used to. You don't know any other. But looking at my other friends complain about one of their parents or when they get two different answers to the same question, I think, I didn't have to go through that mess. I actually liked not having a man in the house. Men have been a negative part of my life starting with my biological father who made a promise that I still remember and I'll never forget. The only great men in my personal life whom I respect to the utmost are my adoptive grandfather, uncles, and my godfather. They were all very loving toward me and always took very good care of me.

Were there challenging and/or difficult aspects of being adopted?

Yes, you're always confused. You are afraid of new changes. At the beginning you feel you don't fit in. There always seemed to be in your mind as a kid, that you were just different. Even if I looked white, there was definitely a piece of the puzzle that's always missing in your mind. You were never at ease and not knowing the same language as everyone else did not help and left you sometimes feeling out of place. But as an adult, I see that all that confusion as a youngster was silly.

Kathy

Kathy, a 31 year-old adoptee, was adopted at the age of fifteen months from Central America.

Were there positive aspects of being adopted?

Yes, there were positive aspects of being adopted. I was given the chance at a wonderful life! I was provided the opportunity to have more wonderful opportunities!

I have a unique history that is fascinating and interesting to others and is a source of pride for me. I only came to appreciate that with age and maturity. And, adoption has become oddly trendy these days! So I guess I'm in vogue!

Were there positive aspects of being adopted by a single person?

There were positives of being adopted by a single person. Although my positives are somewhat silly! I loved the fact that I only had to seek the permission of one parent. I didn't have that second parent to chime in with their ideas and change the mind of the first parent! Also, I didn't have to worry about the possibility that my parents might divorce, or who I'd live with if a separation happened. Step-parents and siblings? Not my problem.

Were there challenging and /or difficult aspects of being adopted?

Yes, there were challenging aspects of being adopted. I'm Hispanic and have beautiful (natural) brown skin! My mother is Caucasian and it's clear that my mother and I are not biologically related. I always hated when people who didn't already know my family would ask why my mother and I, or why my sister and I, looked nothing alike, especially if it was the first meeting. I just found it rude and intrusive, even at a young age! I would usually just tell people that my father was Hispanic and my parents were divorced. Folks understood the language of divorce better than the language of adoption. They'd simply say, "Oh, I see," and move on. At the time, adoption was still foreign to people, definitely not what it is today. The only other difficulty of being adopted isn't directly related to adoption, but is more correlated to being adopted from an impoverished country. I was ill and malnourished when my mom ventured to get me. Like most children who hail from third world countries or poorly funded orphanages, I didn't receive the nurturing, stimulation and nutrition that is important for growth and development. Because of this, my milestones weren't reached on time and I struggled with learning disabilities throughout my school career. For me, this was the most significant challenge of being adopted - and from a poor country. It all turned out very well in the end, I'm pleased to report.

Were there challenging and/or difficult aspects of being adopted by a single person?

There were challenging aspects of being adopted by a single person. The whole "Where's your dad?" thing of course. Also, I only had one parent to seek permission from. Sadly, if my mother didn't give me the response that I was hoping for, there was no possibility that I could appeal to the other parent and try to change the mind of the first parent. That was that! Damn! I'm a HUGE worrier by nature. Always have been. I have a VERY overactive imagination and plan for the worst possible scenario. Flood, fire, famine? I'm on it. Honestly, I own probably five fire extinguishers. Even as a young child I had a concrete understanding that my mother was a single parent with two daughters and one income.

For years I was convinced (due to my own irrational and misguided thinking) that my family was one day away from being homeless and destitute. Could you blame me? Everything that I heard told me that being a single parent meant that you were destined to a life of poverty, instability, and trauma. Sad, huh? Little did I know just how fiscally responsible my mother actually was!

Felicia

Felicia is a 23 year old female who was adopted at six weeks old from South America.

Were there positive aspects of being adopted?

Yes. For one I was given many opportunities in life that I probably wouldn't have had if I were not adopted.

Were there positive aspects of being adopted by a single person?

Yes, I would say that because it is only my mother and I that we are able to have the close relationship that we have.

Were there challenging and/or difficult aspects of being adopted?

I would say that one negative aspect of being adopted was that I missed out on growing up in and experiencing my birth culture.

Were there challenging and/or difficult aspects of being adopted by a single person?

I wouldn't say for me, but more so for my mother. I feel as though it can be easier for two parents when it comes to spending time with children, while single parents aren't able to divide up the time they spend with their children with their spouse.

Liliana

Liliana is a 23 year old young woman adopted at the age of eleven months from Central America.

Were there positive aspects of being adopted?

Yes, I believe that my mother saved me from an extremely impoverished life and gave me the opportunity for a future with endless opportunities. It also sets me apart from others and makes me unique and special.

Were there positive aspects of being adopted by a single person?

I love my mom so much and I don't care that she is single because she provides me with all the love I could possibly attain. I also get everything I need and want. I don't lack anything that two parents could give to me.

Were there challenging and/or difficult aspects of being adopted?

Yes. I can't ever recover from all the feeling I've had related to the experience, and it has forever changed/influenced every aspect of my life. It's difficult to understand unless you have experienced them yourself.

Were there challenging and/or difficult aspects of being adopted by a single person?

Not really because I never knew life with two parents so it didn't affect me. It makes me sad that I didn't have a dad, especially when my friends talk about their dads, but it's OK I guess.

Ana

Ana is a 21 year old female adopted at the age of four from Honduras.

Were there positive aspects of being adopted?

A start of a new life that offered me many more opportunities. A family that loved, supported and could provide for me in times of need.

Were there positive aspects of being adopted by a single person?

Yes, she could be attentive and when needed, completely focused on my needs.

Were there challenging and/or difficult aspects of being adopted?

Yes, not necessarily knowing my background, or, when health or family history was needed, I was always unsure and couldn't always find the answers to the questions I needed.

Were there challenging and/or difficult aspects of being adopted by a single person?

Not always having another parent to do certain activities with. There are little voids that a mother can't fulfill like playing sports with or going camping with.

Roberto

Roberto is 23 years old and was adopted at the age of three from South America.

142

Were there positive aspects of being adopted?

Yes, many. My whole life was changed.

Were there positive aspects of being adopted by a single person?

Yes. One is better than none.

Were there challenging and/or difficult aspects of being adopted?

Yes and no, things were different like all families are. I love the family I have.

Were there challenging and/or difficult aspects of being adopted by a single person?

Yes, because like any family where there is only one parent with two kids things are hard for the family. But we made it through!

Maria

Maria was adopted at the age of three from Central America.

Were there positive aspects of being adopted?

To begin with, I am fortunate to be alive today. And, this must be credited to the fact that I was given a second chance at life through adoption. My adoptive mother, who was single at the time of my adoption, took me away from a life in which I lived under constant threat of danger, namely emotional and physical starvation, as well as the possibility of death due to living within a country besieged by civil war. Therefore, adoption literally and figuratively saved my life. As a survivor, I have been able to cultivate within myself a strong sense of spirituality, a continually lived sense of grace, the patience to wait in hope for insight, clarity and the unfolding of the love of others. I may never have become the person I am today if I had not been given the chance to continue in life both physically and emotionally as an adoptee, I have also been given the unique gift to recognize and respect the many different forms of family that exist today and continue to evolve.

Were there positive aspects of being adopted by a single person?

When my mother decided to begin a family, she had told me that she did so with the desire to share a life that was abundant with good fortune in the form of career success and many deep, intimate and resounding experiences and friendships already enjoyed. She had much to bring us (my biological sister and I) as a well-rounded woman, as well as a person of abundant love, affection and compassion as well as patience. Because she was my only parent, I was able to garner her singly focused love and attention. There was much healing that needed to be done on my part, and with my new mother's help, I learned to trust and love again. Despite the fact that she owned her own very successful company, I never felt as though I was lacking for her time and attention.

Were there challenging or difficult aspects of being adopted by a single parent?

I'd like to mention that I experienced the benefit of living in the same household as my grandparents leaving me fully and lovingly taken care of from the moment I awoke in the morning and excepting the hours I spent in school, until I went to sleep at night. I was also adopted with my biological sister who was and continues to be my greatest confidante and the one person in my life with whom I have survived the trauma of our beginnings. Not only was she a mirror for me, she was also a constant companion having a very strong maternal instinct despite her youth. Needless to say, I enjoyed the benefit of being mothered by many because the responsibility of learning to love and accept a completely new family (no matter how loving), new country and culture was so great. I believe I was fortunate to have to integrate myself into only the family of one parent and not a second one, as well, namely those of whom would have belonged to a father. That other family could safely remain my original (biological) family.

Were there challenging and/or difficult aspects of being adopted?

The greatest difficulty of being adopted was the unchangeable, static aspect of loving and belonging to a mother with whom I did not share a biological connection. This emotional and physical bond will always remain with a mother I may never meet again. It is a missing piece that can never be replaced or mended.

145

Instead, it is always open . But, I have learned that an open heart is also a strong one. From this wound, I have become an artist, a writer, a spiritual seeker and a dreamer. It has taken me nearly three decades to reach this point of self-respect, and I could only have done so by knowing and learning to accept who I am, not who I believed other people wanted me to be, which is something I struggled with as an adopted person, particularly with those within my own adoptive family. I wasn't given the birthright of unconditional love, having instead the responsibility to earn the love of my adoptive family. As a result, I struggled with a lack of self-esteem and continue to do so to this day. As a child, I felt attacked by inadequacy and ostracized as well as alienated by how different I was, internally and externally, from the members of my adoptive family as well as my neighborhood. I continue to suffer with these feelings, along with some significant body image issues.

Tammy

Tammy was adopted at the age of 9 weeks from Texas.

Were there positive aspects of being adopted?

Everything has been positive because I was adopted into such a welcoming and loving family. I wouldn't change anything about my life and I am so grateful for the wonderful opportunities and experiences I've had.

Were there positive aspects of being adopted by a single person?

For several years it was just me and my mother so we were able to become really close. She was and is my best friend.

Were there challenging and /or difficult aspects of being adopted?

No, there weren't challenges or difficulties because my mother was always very open with me about my adoption and my biological family. My family is the one that has raised me since I was nine weeks old.

Were there challenging and /or difficult aspects of being adopted by a single person?

No, our family has evolved over the years but for 11 years of my life I was raised by a single mom and I don't feel like I missed out on anything. Speaking for myself I do believe she did a wonderful job.

Jorge

Jorge is a 29 year old male, adopted at the age of two from Central America.

Were there positive aspects of being adopted?

Absolutely! I can think of many but the most important aspects are the opportunity for a life, the opportunity of being loved unconditionally when my biological parents couldn't. Finding God and meeting a woman who was chosen for me by God who will unquestionably never be duplicated! Having the chance

147

to do the same as a father to my daughter. Giving my daughter what I never knew- a father. By being her father I fill the void in myself!!

Were there positive aspects of being adopted by a single person?

It built character. What was blind to me in my younger years was revealed later in life, which would be a learning experience that I would hold tight to my heart! Knowing that no matter the tribulations one woman stood by me while others ran or gave up, that's **strength**!

Were there challenging and/or difficult aspects of being adopted?

Yes, so many questions not enough answers, lonely tears, feelings of abandonment which lead to trust issues and to great walls built so high that even I couldn't see over them. Anger and self-hatred. Where do I belong? Emptiness, not knowing who I look like or the traits that were passed down from whom? Opening up, **finding me.** Just being adopted, growing up as a little boy and being a man now but still having that little vulnerable boy inside me who sits curled up in the dark whom I've tried to protect and kept away from everyone until now, not knowing if another person will ever know my experience.

Lia

Lia was adopted at three months old from India.

148

Were there positive aspects of being adopted?

Yes, there were many positive aspects of being adopted because I was given a new life and a chance.

Were there positive aspects of being adopted by a single person?

Yes, my mother was a single parent until later in my life. She had strong connections with family and friends so I had a good web of family and support.

Were there challenging and/or difficult aspects of being adopted?

There is always this thought or question of what happened, and the uncertainty of where I came from and who I am. I have an identity that has grown with me since I was little, but knowing fully who I am won't be known because it's part of being adopted.

Were there challenging and/or difficult aspects of being adopted by a single person?

No. She gave me the love and care and support as two parents would. She had a strong support system through friends and family.

Barbara

Barbara was adopted at 11 days old from New York.

Were there positive aspects of being adopted?

Yes, the most positive aspect for me would be ending up with a great family who love and support me. I also have a great family story, my mom always told me "love makes a family" and this is something I strongly believe in.

Were there positive aspects of being adopted by a single person?

Yes, being adopted by a single mom allowed my family to grow and blossom. For example, first it was just my mom and me, and then my mom met my other mom. Then my new mom gave birth to my little sister. Later my moms cross-adopted my sister and I. This story all started with a 40 year-old single mom.

Were there challenging and/or difficult aspects of being adopted?

For me the most challenging part was my birth-father who felt he needed to be part of my life. My birth-mother put me up for adoption without telling my birth-father. Therefore my family and I have had to deal with many legal issues with him.

Were there challenging and/or difficult aspects of being adopted by a single person?

I only had a single parent during my early years so I don't remember how difficult it was.

In conclusion

The above responses are heartfelt and compelling. They are as diverse as the individuals who wrote them, and we believe they have valuable information to share with us. They are unique individuals who were willing to come forward and share a piece of their life experience. We include this chapter to provide the perspectives of ten individuals who wanted to share their stories.

APPENDIX

Books for Young Children in Single Adoptive Families

Books are fun to read. Books read aloud or together are a great way to share time. But books also can help children make sense of their own lives. Particularly those parts of their lives that they may have questions about but don't always feel like talking about. Being adopted, being raised by a single parent, being raised by a gay or lesbian parent – while more common than 25 years ago when our children arrived home - can still cause children to feel different than their peers.

Books that can be read over and over from a young age can help children gain insight, express feelings and develop understanding about their own family situation. Reading about children who may struggle with some of the same feelings they do or who come from similar backgrounds can help them label, express, and validate their own thoughts and feelings.

When problems arise such as those questions on the playground: "Where are your *real* parents? Why didn't your parents keep you?" books can give children a repertoire of responses to deal with the situation.

We have found many books that have provided guidance. Following is a list of books you may enjoy.

The Family Book by Todd Parr (preschool – Grade 2). This book, with its bright childlike pictures, introduces the reader to many different kinds of families including families formed through adoption as well as single parent families and gay and lesbian headed families.

Whose is a Family by Robert Scutch (ages 4 – 8) also includes many different family make-ups from various ethnicities. It ends with a blank page where children can draw a picture of their own family. In both of these books the message is the same – whatever the makeup of the family it is the love and commitment to each other that makes a family.

A Mother for Choco by Keiko Kasza (preschool –K).This is a classic tale of Choco, a yellow bird with a blue beak and striped feet, who goes searching for a mother. He tries various animals, none of whom work out, until he meets Mrs. Bear. Mrs. Bear, who appears to be single, brings him home to join her other children – a hippo, an alligator, and a pig. The message that families are created from love and sharing, and not from superficial appearances, is depicted in bright watercolor illustrations

The Little Green Goose by Adele Sansone (K – grade 3) has a similar message – what makes a family is not looking the same but sharing and caring. In this story, Mr. Goose longs for a baby. Finally Daisy the dog finds an egg for him and Mr. Goose builds a nest for it.

154

At last a scaly-skinned, spiky-tailed "green goose" hatches and calls him Mama. But the hens in the barnyard taunt him and tell him "Mr. Goose can't be your real Mother." The green goose tries to find a mother that looks like him only to realize where he truly belongs.

Along similar lines, *The Lamb-a-Roo* (ages 2 and up) by Diana Kimpton tells the story of a lonely lamb who wants a mother and a sad kangaroo who wants a baby of her own. They find each other and become a family until the lamb realizes he is different from other kangaroo kids and attempts to fit in, with some funny consequences.

Little Miss Spider by David Kirk (ages 3 and up) is part of a series of Little Miss Spider books. In this story Miss Spider has popped out of her egg and wonders where her mother is. A passing beetle offers her help and they go off searching together. Miss Spider never finds her biological mother but adopts Betty the Beetle as her mother.

Pablo's Tree by Pat Mora (ages 4 – 8) is about five year old Pablo who looks forward to seeing his grandfather on his birthday. When his Mama (a single woman) had first told her father she was going to adopt a baby, he went out and bought a special tree for his grandson. Every year he decorates the tree for Pablo's birthday.

I Love You Like Crazy Cakes by Rose Lewis (ages 4 – 8). This book is about a single mother who adopts a little girl from China. It is followed by a sequel: *Every Year on Your Birthday* in which a single mother describes her daughters first five years, beginning with her birth in China and ending with her celebrating her 5th birthday with a picnic overlooking a dragon-boat festival.

The Red Blanket by Eliza Thomas (preschool – grade 2) is another vibrantly illustrated book by a single mother who adopted from China. It tells the tale of the red blanket the mother buys to comfort her new daughter.

The Best Single Mother in the World: How I was Adopted by Mary Zisk (preschool – K). A mother and child share in the telling of the story of an adoption. It tells of the mother's search for a child to adopt, including meeting the child's birth-mother.

Two Birthdays for Beth by Gay Lynn Cronin (ages 4 – 8). This is a story of domestic adoption by a single African-American woman.

For those who want a customized story of their child's adoption there is a great resource at Adoptshoppe.com. You send them the information you want in the book and they create it especially for you.

RESOURCES

General Resources

Adopting.com – One of the best overall adoption sites. Adopting.com includes information and support, parent profiles as well as waiting-child photo listings and descriptions of children awaiting adoption.

ACONE (Adoption Community of New England) – Advocacy, Education, Resources and Support for all members of the adoption community. Annual Conference.

Adoption.org – Another good site for information and resources includes adoption articles, blogs and forums.

Adoption Network Law Center – Focus on domestic Adoption. Founded by adoptive parents.

Adoptive Families – Award-winning national adoption magazine.

American Academy of Adoption Attorneys – Helps disseminate information on ethical adoption practices. Publishes member directory.

Child Welfare Information Gateway – Focuses on Adoption from the US foster care system.

Center for Family Connections – Educational and clinical resources. Based in Cambridge, MA, CFFC also does trainings nationally and internationally.

Creating A Family – Resources on adoption and infertility. Weekly radio show.

Dave Thomas Foundation – Focuses on adoption from US foster care system.

Evan Donaldson Adoption Institute – Provides research, education and advocacy. Examines relevant issues, laws and practice pertaining to single as well as LGBT adoption. Reviews relevant studies over the last several decades.

National Adoption Information Clearinghouse – Focuses on services for children in the US foster care system.

North American Council on Adoptable Children – Advocates for the rights of waiting children for permanent placements in loving adoptive homes. Concentrates on children with special needs.

RainbowKids.com – An international adoption online magazine. Includes photo listings of children.

The Ties Program – Sponsors adoptive family homeland journeys.

US State Department Office of Children's Issues – International adoption resources.

Resources for Singles

Although the above resources include information and resources for singles the following are specifically for singles

Adopting on Your Own: The Complete Guide to Adopting as a Single Parent by Lee Varon. Farrar Straus and Giroux, 2000.

Forever Families: 7 Stories of Single Parent Adoption – DVD produced by Sherry Fine. 2008.

Choosing Single Motherhood: The Thinking Woman's Guide by Mikki Morrissette. Focuses on having children by birth but includes some adoption information.

Grants for Single Moms – Resources for single Mothers including grants and information to help become a single mom through domestic adoption or foster care.

Single Mothers by Choice: A Guidebook for Women Who are Considering or Have Chosen Motherhood by Jane Mattes. Includes information on adoption.

Single Mothers by Choice is also an organization that provides information and support for single women who are considering or have chosen motherhood by conception or adoption. It was founded in 1981 by Jane Mattes LCSW, a psychotherapist and single mother by choice. Members of Single Mothers by Choice are from across the US as well as Canada, Europe and beyond. Provides forums and quarterly publication.

SPACE (Single Parent Adoption of Children Everywhere) – Support group in the New England area for singles who have adopted.

Further resources for singles can be found on **Adopting.com** which has many country-specific online support groups, listservs and forums for singles.

LGBT Resources:

Many LGBT Resources can be found on **Adopting.com**.

COLAGE – Children of Lesbians and Gays Everywhere. Support organization for LGBT families.

Daddy & Papa – A one-hour documentary about gay families, formed mainly through adoption. Follows four families.

Families Like Mine – Information for children in LGBT Families and link to their book: **Families Like Mine: Children of Gay Parents Tell it Like it is**.

LGBT Communities & Adoption: Courting an Untapped Resource – Study Published by The North American Council on Adoptable Children at www.nacan.org.

info@rainbowfamilies.org – support and resources for LGBT families. The **Rainbow Families** organization can be found in cities in several other countries. Information can be found if you Google rainbowfamilies.org.

Families Like Ours – Focuses on LGBT families adopting from foster care.

Exploring Resources for Children – 2011 study by the Evan B. Donaldson Adoption Institute which reports on a four-year study of adoption by gay men and lesbians at www.adoptioninstitute.org.

Gay Adoption Basics – Helpful entry at About.com

LGBT Families – Resource for LGBT community seeking to expand their families though adoption, foster care, surrogacy and fertility at lgbtfamilies.info

Rainbow Rumpus – online magazine for children of LGBT Families. Sections for teachers, parents and friends.

therainbowbabies.com – information for LGBT families